Keith M. K...
Elizabeth A. Segal
Editors

Poverty and Inequality in the Latin American-U.S. Borderlands: Implications of U.S. Interventions

Poverty and Inequality in the Latin American-U. S. Borderlands: Implications of U.S. Interventions has been co-published simultaneously as *Journal of Poverty*, Volume 8, Number 4 2004.

Pre-publication
REVIEWS,
COMMENTARIES,
EVALUATIONS . . .

"CHALLENGES OVERSIMPLI-FYING MODELS OF NORTH-ERN AFFLUENCE AND SOUTHERN POVERTY. . . . The editors' imagination of 'borderlands' between the U.S. and Latin American nations in a use fully broad manner helps frame the chapters which engage conceptual borders in interesting ways: between experiences and neoliberal definitions of poverty; between counterinsurgency tactics, gender relations, and government profits; between definitions of activism and terrorism in Vieques, Puerto Rico; between communities linked by migration; and between sustainable development and commodified environments."

Ann Kingsolver, PhD
Associate Professor of Anthropology
and Interim Director
Latin American Studies Program

More pre-publication
REVIEWS, COMMENTARIES, EVALUATIONS . . .

"**M**UST READING FOR STUDENTS concerned with Latin American relations as well as for students of poverty and inequality. This is a powerful book that increases the sensitivity of those who study and work with Latin American populations. M. Gabriela Torres describes how counter insurgency and governmental propaganda in Guatemala increased gender and ethnic inequalities. Lucy Luccisano argues that neo-liberal interventions such as cash transfers for human capital development not only reduce poverty but at the same time serve as techniques to control individual conduct. Nora Haenn examines subsidy programs in southern Mexico and concluded that those programs reinforced a continuing rural poverty. Rebecca Burwell highlights the effect of the U.S. embargo on Cuba and the struggle of Cuban women. Maria Vidal de Haymes and Mauricio Cifuentes reflect on Cuban and Mexican immigrant experiences. And Carmen I. Aponte describes how Puerto Ricans were able to employ civil disobedience and solidarity in removing the U.S. Navy, which performed military maneuvers there for many years, from Vieques, Puerto Rico."

Tony Tripodi, DSW
Dean and Professor
College of Social Work
The Ohio State University

The Haworth Press, Inc.
New York

Poverty and Inequality in the Latin American-U.S. Borderlands: Implications of U.S. Interventions

Poverty and Inequality in the Latin American-U.S. Borderlands: Implications of U.S. Interventions has been co-published simultaneously as *Journal of Poverty*, Volume 8, Number 4 2004.

The *Journal of Poverty* Monographic "Separates"

Below is a list of "separates," which in serials librarianship means a special issue simultaneously published as a special journal issue or double-issue *and* as a "separate" hardbound monograph. (This is a format which we also call a "DocuSerial.")

"Separates" are published because specialized libraries or professionals may wish to purchase a specific thematic issue by itself in a format which can be separately cataloged and shelved, as opposed to

purchasing the journal on an on-going basis. Faculty members may also more easily consider a "separate" for classroom adoption.

"Separates" are carefully classified separately with the major book jobbers so that the journal tie-in can be noted on new book order slips to avoid duplicate purchasing.

You may wish to visit Haworth's website at . . .

http://www.HaworthPress.com

. . . to search our online catalog for complete tables of contents of these separates and related publications.

You may also call 1-800-HAWORTH (outside US/Canada: 607-722-5857), or Fax 1-800-895-0582 (out - side US/Canada: 607-771-0012), or e-mail at:

docdelivery@haworthpress.com

Poverty and Inequality in the Latin American-U.S. Borderlands: Implications of U.S. Interventions, edited by Keith M. Kilty, PhD, and Elizabeth A. Segal, PhD (Vol. 8, No. 4, 2004).*"Must reading for students concerned with Latin American relations as well as for students of poverty and inequality." (Tony Tripodi, DSW, Dean and Professor, College of Social Work, The Ohio State University)*

Rediscovering the Other America: The Continuing Crisis of Poverty and Inequality in the United States, edited by Keith M. Kilty, PhD, and Elizabeth A. Segal, PhD (Vol. 7, No. 1/2, 2003). *"An extremely important book for social scientists, social workers, and healthcare practitioners." (Tony Tripodi, DSW, Dean and Professor, College of Social Work, The Ohio State University)*

Latino Poverty in the New Century: Inequalities, Challenges and Barriers, edited by Maria Vidal de Haymes, PhD, Keith M. Kilty, PhD, and Elizabeth A. Segal, PhD (Vol. 4, No. 1/2, 2000). *Provides social workers and policymakers with wide-ranging analyses of some of the pressing issues and social policies that highlight the impact of inequality and poverty in relation to available resources and opportunities.*

Pressing Issues of Inequality and American Indian Communities, edited by Elizabeth A. Segal, PhD, and Keith M. Kilty, PhD (Vol. 2, No. 4, 1998). *"Useful in its illustrations of the different impact of social welfare policy on diverse communities. . . . An important and valuable resource." (Sandra S. Butler, PhD, Associate Professor, School of Social Work, University of Maine)*

Income Security and Public Assistance for Women and Children, edited by Keith M. Kilty, PhD, Virginia E. Richardson, PhD, MSW, and Elizabeth A. Segal, PhD, MSW (Vol. 1, No. 2, 1997). *"Offers valuable insight and direction for ensuring income security and public assistance for women and children who are in poverty and gives them an opportunity to present what they believe they need to have in order to become independent." (American Public Welfare Association)*

Poverty and Inequality in the Latin American-U.S. Borderlands: Implications of U.S. Interventions

Keith M. Kilty
Elizabeth A. Segal
Editors

Poverty and Inequality in the Latin American U.S. Borderlands: Implications of U.S. Interventions has been co-published simultaneously as *Journal of Poverty*, Volume 8, Number 4 2004.

The Haworth Press, Inc.

New York • London • Victoria (AU)
www.HaworthPress.com

Poverty and Inequality in the Latin American-U.S. Borderlands: Implications of U.S. Interventions has been co-published simultaneously as *Journal of Poverty*™, Volume 8, Number 4 2004.

The development, preparation, and publication of this work has been undertaken with great care. However, the publisher, employees, editors, and agents of The Haworth Press and all imprints of The Haworth Press, Inc., including The Haworth Medical Press® and Pharmaceutical Products Press®, are not responsible for any errors contained herein or for consequences that may ensue from use of materials or information contained in this work. Opinions expressed by the author(s) are not necessarily those of The Haworth Press, Inc. With regard to case studies, identities and circumstances of individuals discussed herein have been changed to protect confidentiality. Any resemblance to actual persons, living or dead, is entirely coincidental.

Cover design by Jennifer M. Gaska

Library of Congress Cataloging-in-Publication Data

Poverty and inequality in the Latin American-U.S. borderlands : implications of U.S. interventions / Keith M. Kilty, Elizabeth A. Segal, editors.
     p. cm.
     "Co-published simultaneously as Journal of Poverty, Volume 8, Number 4 2004."
     Includes bibliographical references and index.
     ISBN 0-7890-2751-8 (hard cover : alk. paper) – ISBN 0-7890-2752-6 (soft cover : alk. paper)
     1. Poverty–Mexico. 2. Poverty–Cuba. 3. Poverty–Guatemala. 4. Poverty–Puerto Rico. 5. United States–Foreign relations–Latin America. 6. Latin America–Foreign relations–United States. I. Kilty, Keith M. (Keith Michael), 1946- II. Segal, Elizabeth A. III. Journal of poverty v. 8, no. 4 (Special number)
HC130.P6P683 2005
339.4'6'0972–dc22
                                  2004028899

Indexing, Abstracting & Website/Internet Coverage

This section provides you with a list of major indexing & abstracting services and other tools for bibliographic access. That is to say, each service began covering this periodical during the year noted in the right column. Most Websites which are listed below have indicated that they will either post, disseminate, compile, archive, cite or alert their own Website users with research-based content from this work. (This list is as current as the copyright date of this publication.)

Abstracting, Website/Indexing Coverage . . . . Year When Coverage Began

- *Alzheimer's Disease Education & Referral Center (ADEAR)* **1997**
- *Business Source Corporate: coverage of nearly 3,350 quality magazines and journals; designed to meet the diverse information needs of corporations; EBSCO Publishing <http://www.epnet.com/corporate/bsourcecorp.asp>* **2001**
- *CareData: the database supporting social care management and practice <http://www.elsc.org.uk/caredata/caredata.htm>* . . . **1997**
- *Criminal Justice Abstracts* **1997**
- *EBSCOhost Electronic Journals Service (EJS) <http://ejournals.ebsco.com>* **2001**
- *Educational Research Abstracts (ERA) (online database) <http://www.tandf.co.uk/era>* **2002**
- *Family Index Database <http://www.familyscholar.com>* **2002**
- *Family & Society Studies Worldwide <http://www.nisc.com>* **1997**
- *FINDEX <http://www.publist.com>* **1999**
- *FRANCIS. INIST/CNRS <http://www.inist.fr>* **1998**
- *Guide to Social Science & Religion in Periodical Literature* **1997**
- *IBZ International Bibliography of Periodical Literature <http://www.saur.de>* **2001**

(continued)

*Special Bibliographic Notes related to special journal issues (separates)
and indexing/abstracting:*

- indexing/abstracting services in this list will also cover material in any
  "separate" that is co-published simultaneously with Haworth's special
  thematic journal issue or DocuSerial. Indexing/abstracting usually covers
  material at the article/chapter level.
- monographic co-editions are intended for either non-subscribers or libraries
  which intend to purchase a second copy for their circulating collections.
- monographic co-editions are reported to all jobbers/wholesalers/approval
  plans. The source journal is listed as the "series" to assist the prevention of
  duplicate purchasing in the same manner utilized for books-in-series.
- to facilitate user/access services all indexing/abstracting services are encouraged to utilize the co-indexing entry note indicated at the bottom of the
  first page of each article/chapter/contribution.
- this is intended to assist a library user of any reference tool (whether print,
  electronic, online, or CD-ROM) to locate the monographic version if the library has purchased this version but not a subscription to the source journal.
- individual articles/chapters in any Haworth publication are also available
  through the Haworth Document Delivery Service (HDDS).

ABOUT THE EDITORS

Keith M. Kilty, PhD, is Professor in the College of Social Work at Ohio State University in Columbus and co-editor of the *Journal of Poverty*. He has published or presented more than 50 papers and is an editorial reviewer for *ALCOHOLISM: Clinical and Experimental Research*, the *Journal of Studies on Alcohol*, and the *American Education Research Journal*, and Assistant Editor for the *Journal of Drug Issues*. Dr. Kilty is a member of the Society for the Study of Social Problems and was Chair of the Poverty, Class, and Inequality Division. He is also Treasurer of the Bertha Capen Reynolds Society.

Elizabeth A. Segal, PhD, MSW, is Professor in the College of Social Work at Arizona State University in Tempe and co-editor of the *Journal of Poverty*. She has made many presentations and conducted workshops and seminars on various issues concerning social work and is the author of many articles, book chapters, book reviews, proceedings, and reports. She served as a policy analyst in Washington, DC as a Fellow of the American Association for the Advancement of Science. Dr. Segal is a member of the National Association of Social Workers, the Council on Social Work Education, and the Bertha Capen Reynolds Society.

Poverty and Inequality in the Latin American-U.S. Borderlands: Implications of U.S. Interventions

CONTENTS

THOUGHTS ON POVERTY AND INEQUALITY

Poverty and Inequality in the Latin American-U.S. Borderlands: Implications of U.S. Interventions: Introduction

Keith M. Kilty
Elizabeth A. Segal

Throughout its history, the United States has viewed itself as having a special dominion over the countries that make up Latin America. Typically, this vision has been described in terms of the U.S. having a unique "protectorate" mission for the western hemisphere. This vision was first expressed in what came to be called the Monroe Doctrine. In his annual address to Congress in 1823, President James Monroe declared the Americas off-limits to European powers, with the exception of already existing European colonies. According to Chasteen (2001, p. 202), "The Monroe Doctrine had remained mostly bluster for a half century. Still, along with a superior attitude, the idea that the Americas, North and South, share a special relationship became an enduring assumption of U.S. policy toward Latin America." As U.S. military power grew, especially its Navy, in the late nineteenth century, the Doctrine

Keith M. Kilty, PhD, is affiliated with Ohio State University.
Elizabeth A. Segal, PhD, is affiliated with Arizona State University.

[Haworth co-indexing entry note]: "Poverty and Inequality in the Latin American-U.S. Borderlands: Implications of U.S. Interventions: Introduction." Kilty, Keith M., and Elizabeth A. Segal. Co-published simultaneously in *Journal of Poverty* (The Haworth Press, Inc.) Vol. 8, No. 4, 2004, pp. 1-5; and: *Poverty and Inequality in the Latin American-U.S. Borderlands: Implications of U.S. Interventions* (ed: Keith M. Kilty, and Elizabeth A. Segal) The Haworth Press, Inc., 2004, pp. 1-5. Single or multiple copies of this article are available for a fee from The Haworth Document Delivery Service [1-800-HAWORTH, 9:00 a.m. - 5:00 p.m. (EST). E-mail address: docdelivery@haworthpress.com].

http://www.haworthpress.com/web/JPOV
Digital Object Identifier: 10.1300/J134v08n04_01

1

became much more than bluster. During the presidency of Theodore Roosevelt, this policy saw increasing enforcement throughout the Americas, by gunboat on the sea and by marines on the land–the "Roosevelt Corollary."

The Monroe Doctrine has always been largely self-serving to the United States, but it has provided a justification for its interventions throughout Central and South America and the Caribbean. While the U.S. saw itself as a protector of Latin America from the colonial powers of Europe, it also came to see itself in the role of a protector of Latin Americans from themselves. It was during the presidency of Theodore Roosevelt that U.S. policy crystallized:

> Roosevelt thought that the U.S. government should no longer tolerate European interventions. Yet, he believed, incompetent Latin American governments would occasionally need correction "by some civilized nation." During these same years, cartoons in U.S. newspapers often showed Uncle Sam dealing with Cuba, Puerto Rico, Nicaragua, and other countries caricatured as naughty "little black Sambos." Uncle Sam was sometimes shown as a stern but benevolent teacher, reluctantly whipping these childish pranksters. Likewise, under the Roosevelt Corollary it became U.S. policy to discipline Latin American countries militarily when "required" by international trade and finance. And it was required fairly often. By the close of the neocolonial period in 1929, 40 percent of all U.S. international investments were in Latin America. (Chasteen, 2001, p. 203)

A century later, these beliefs and attitudes about Latin America remain entrenched in the thinking of North Americans–both policy-makers and ordinary citizens. The same ideas that were used to justify the war with Spain in 1898 continue to serve as justifications for U.S. interventions in the region–whether in Guatemala in the 1950s, Cuba and the Dominican Republic in the 1960s, Chile in the 1970s, Nicaragua and El Salvador in the 1980s, Colombia and Peru in the 1990s, or Venezuela and Brazil in the first decade of this century.

Poverty and inequality are endemic problems throughout the Americas. While they may be more extreme in many parts of Latin America than in the U.S., these problems are persistent and interconnected throughout this hemisphere. Our goal in this collection of papers is to examine poverty and inequality in the borderlands of Latin America, with a particular focus on the implications of U.S. interventions, be they economic, political, social, and/or military. Different countries have their own unique histories, but an understanding of poverty and inequality in the Americas needs to examine the connections between the U.S. and Latin America. Sometimes, the impact of U.S. interventions is subtle and hidden; at other times, it is more direct and visible. This is especially true in the so-called "borderlands."

We use the term "borderlands" in a broader sense than is often the case in studies of Latin America. Traditionally, the term has been used to refer to the border between the U.S. and Mexico (e.g., Anzaldua, 1999; Martinez, 1996). Certainly, that boundary is an important one, particularly in regard to immigration issues (Kilty & Vidal de Haymes, 2000). At the same time, boundaries are artificial devices that serve the interests of governments and ruling elites but not necessarily the people themselves. The U.S.-Mexico border has been porous, but so have the rest of the official boundaries of the U.S. Historically, Latin American migrants, documented or otherwise, have entered not only along the Mexico-U.S. divide, but at other entry points as well–particularly Puerto Ricans and Cubans. Furthermore, in recent years, the Mexico-U.S. border has seen the crossing not just of migrants from Mexico but from many other parts of Latin America. That can clearly be seen in the variety of cultures represented among Latino/as in this country (Heyck, 1994). For our purposes, we identify borderlands (including the bodies of water) as separating the U.S. from its nearby neighbors, including Mexico, Cuba, Puerto Rico, and Guatemala–the countries represented in this volume. A broader concept of borderlands is necessary, in light of the 9/11 attacks on the U.S., which have impacted on immigration and border relations. Since 2001, there has been increasing anxiety and hostility toward immigrants in this country as well as increasing actions and border surveillance by immigration authorities (Vidal de Haymes & Kilty, 2003).

We start with Guatemala, a country that has seen a variety of U.S. interventions, particularly in the second half of the twentieth century. The CIA engineered a military takeover of the Guatemalan government in 1954 that dramatically affected the lives and well-being of its citizens. Many thousands of Guatemalans, particularly its indigenous population, died (Chasteen, 2001), and a strong resistance movement developed. Torres describes the brutal response of the Guatemalan government as it developed into what she describes as a "counterinsurgent state." The Guatemalan officials drew from a variety of cultural exports from the U.S. in creating a fear of the insurgency movement, including anti-communism rhetoric as well as fundamentalist Christianity. Gender became an important aspect of government propaganda in terms of identifying the villains–i.e., those who were identified as threatening the fabric of Guatemalan society.

Another important cultural export from the North has been neo-liberal economic policy, which focuses the problem of poverty on the poor–in many ways, a newly revised version of "blaming the victim." In the U.S., poverty policy has increasingly focused on the poor themselves as the root problem. Simply giving people aid creates dependency rather than independence. In her paper, Luccisano focuses on Mexico's Progresa Program, which ostensibly provided assistance to families, but which in fact provided new forms for controlling individual behavior. The poor need to become responsible for the choices they make, according to this line of reasoning. Is this a form of poverty reduction, or a mechanism of control, particularly for women?

At the end of the Spanish-American War of 1898, Puerto Rico became a colony of the United States, even though Spain had given it independence the previous year. This country has never seemed able to decide exactly how to deal with this colony and its often unruly people. Not all Latin Americanists identify Puerto Rico as a part of "Latin America" because of its unique status as a colony of the United States. Its citizens may be officially "American" and possess U.S. citizenship, but that does not mean they are treated as such, either on the island or on the mainland. Aponte shows how resistance to U.S. rule has manifested itself in the recent past, with the protests over the use of the island of Vieques as a bombing and gunnery range for the U.S. Navy. A profound struggle to demilitarize the island brought many Puerto Ricans and supporters together in collective actions that ultimately led the U.S. Navy to abandon the island. This paper shows how civil disobedience, social action, and solidarity became the tools to achieve social justice.

For over 40 years, Cuba has felt the impact of U.S. military, economic, and political intervention. It has faced a trade embargo intended to bring its "communist" government to collapse. Yet its government has survived the end of the Cold War and the anti-communist rhetoric of that era–the justification behind many U.S. involvements in Latin America. As Burwell describes in her paper, making ends meet in a constant state of hardship has been difficult for many Cuban citizens. Yet the citizens of that country–especially its women–are nothing if not resilient and have found ways to put food on the tables for their families. Once again, we see how gender is an important component of adaptation to the impact of U.S. policy. Further, we see how the Cuban government helps its people in acquiring the basic necessities of life, in contrast to the U.S. government and the governments of many Latin

American nations, which apply neo-liberal privatization policies supposedly as methods of "poverty reduction."

We return to the issue of neo-liberal policies in Mexico in the paper by Haenn. In this case, the focus is on rural poverty, and government programs, related to education and to environment, which presumably will lead to poverty reduction. The question again is how programs are conceptualized and how they are carried out–are their implicit assumptions and goals that differ from the explicit goals and assumptions stated by the architects of programs? How is poverty conceived in the neo-liberal context, and can those conceptions reduce it, particularly given the constraints on delivering assistance in rural Mexico?

While many of these papers try to give voice to the people who are directly affected by poverty and inequality in Latin America, we also include two papers that bring a more personal edge to these problems in our "Thoughts on Poverty and Inequality" section. Vidal de Haymes' paper reflects the experiences of a Cubana brought to the U.S. as a refugee as a young child. Her life experience was shaped by the conflict between the U.S. and the Castro-led government in Cuba. Cifuentes' paper focuses on clients in a program for Mexican immigrants in Chicago. Many of the people who participate in this outreach program (C.I.E.L.O.) are undocumented (scurrilously labeled as "illegals" by some) immigrants trying to find a way out of the deeply-entrenched poverty in their homeland–poverty often exacerbated by U.S. policies, such as NAFTA. These poignant tales hopefully bring a human face to poverty and inequality in the borderlands.

REFERENCES

Anzaldua, G. (1999). *Borderlands/La Frontera: The new mestiza.* (2nd ed.). San Francisco: Aunt Lute Books.

Chasteen, J. C. (2001). *Born in blood and fire: A concise history of Latin America.* New York: W. W. Norton.

Heyck, D. L. D. (1994). *Barrios and borderlands: Cultures of Latinos and Latinas in the United States.* New York: Routledge.

Kilty, K. M., & Vidal de Haymes, M. Racism, nativism, and exclusion: Public policy, immigration, and the Latino experience in the U.S. *Journal of Poverty, 4* (1/2), 1-25.

Martinez, O. J. (ed.) (1996). *U.S.-Mexico borderlands: Historical and contemporary perspectives.* Wilmington, DE: Scholarly Resources.

Vidal de Haymes, M., & Kilty, K. M. (2003). Trends in Latino family immigration, legal status, and settlement patterns: Implications for social welfare. Paper presented at the Annual Meeting of the Society for the Study of Social Problems, Atlanta (August).

Constructing the Threat of Insurgency: Inherent Inequalities in the Development of the Guatemalan Counterinsurgent State

M. Gabriela Torres

SUMMARY. The counterinsurgent state is the continuing legacy of political violence that afflicted Guatemala for the last thirty years of the 20th century. As the Guatemalan counterinsurgent state entrenched itself into the country's social fabric, it promoted a highly unequal social, cultural, and economic development that still plagues the country today.

The paper explores how economic, gender and ethnic inequalities were heightened by the integration of counterinsurgency violence into the everyday functioning of the Guatemalan state. Focusing on the processes through which the insurgent threat was promoted, the paper analyses the lasting effects of counterinsurgency-fuelled social change in Guatemala. *[Article copies available for a fee from The Haworth Document Delivery Service: 1-800-HAWORTH. E-mail address: <docdelivery@haworthpress.*

M. Gabriela Torres is a Social Sciences and Humanities Research Council of Canada Post-Doctoral Fellow (Department of Sociology and Anthropology, University of Windsor). She received her PhD (Social Anthropology) from York University, her MA (Applied Anthropology) from the Latin American Faculty of Social Sciences (Flacso-Ecuador), and her BA (International Relations) from the University of British Columbia.

Address correspondence to: 58 Cornwall Street, Toronto, Ontario, Canada, M5A-4K5.

Social Sciences and Humanities Research Council of Canada, York University, and the Ontario Graduate Scholarship Program provided funding for this project.

[Haworth co-indexing entry note]: "Constructing the Threat of Insurgency: Inherent Inequalities in the Development of the Guatemalan Counterinsurgent State." Torres, M. Gabriela. Co-published simultaneously in *Journal of Poverty* (The Haworth Press, Inc.) Vol. 8, No. 4, 2004, pp. 7-29; and: *Poverty and Inequality in the Latin American-U.S. Borderlands: Implications of U.S. Interventions* (ed: Keith M. Kilty, and Elizabeth A. Segal) The Haworth Press, Inc., 2004, pp. 7-29. Single or multiple copies of this article are available for a fee from The Haworth Document Delivery Service [1-800-HAWORTH, 9:00 a.m. - 5:00 p.m. (EST). E-mail address: docdelivery@haworthpress.com].

http://www.haworthpress.com/web/JPOV
Digital Object Identifier: 10.1300/J134v08n04_02

KEYWORDS. Violence, Guatemala, inequality, counterinsurgency, state formation, gender, and ethnicity

The entrenchment of a counterinsurgent state is the continuing legacy of political violence that afflicted Guatemala for the last thirty years of the 20th century. The inequalities promoted by counterinsurgent states are pervasive, long lasting, and always go beyond obvious constraints placed on a country's political development. Exploring the ways that counterinsurgency policies can affect a country's cultural, economic, and political development is vital given today's current world context where counterinsurgency regimes are, again, being promoted as a requisite of fledgling democracies throughout the world.

From the outset, the Guatemalan counterinsurgent state capitalized on pre-existing social fissures. As the Guatemalan counterinsurgent state entrenched itself into the country's social fabric, it promoted a highly unequal social, cultural, and economic development that still plagues the country today. This paper explores how gender, ethnic, and economic inequalities were heightened by the integration of counterinsurgency violence into the everyday functioning of the Guatemalan state. Focusing on the processes through which the insurgent threat was promoted and the economic consequences of military strategies, this paper analyses the lasting effects of counterinsurgency-fuelled social change in Guatemala.

WHAT IS COUNTERINSURGENCY?

Counterinsurgency operations are state-sponsored, primarily military, actions taken to prevent the establishment of a military force that could pose a challenge to a state's ability to govern. The counterinsurgency strategies employed by Guatemalan military governments during *La Violencia* included, in addition to military offensives, different types of military and psychological operations aimed at affecting the political, economic, social, cultural, and religious order of Guatemala. Ostensibly, counterinsurgency strategies are designed to be used as deterrents to citizen behaviour that could be construed as putting the ruling construction of the "nation-state" in jeopardy. In Guatemala–as was the case of other Latin American military dictatorships (Marchak, 1999)–counterinsurgency operations were designed to operate, not only to realize the destruction of a small armed insurgency, but to ensure that any ideological threats to the military elites' vision of a nation-state were also destroyed.

Counterinsurgency policies in Guatemala are characterized as a series of strategies through which the Guatemalan Armed Forces aimed to construct a nation state that best fit its long-term interests in acquiring and retaining a privileged position of political and economic power. As such, counterinsurgency policies need to be examined as socio-economic policies of governance whose effects extend beyond their traditional military context into the promotion of different levels of political, social, cultural, and economic inequality.

THE ORGANIZATION OF COUNTERINSURGENCY POLICIES IN GUATEMALA

The deployment of counterinsurgency policies in Guatemala occurred within the context of U.S. cold war interests in the region. U.S. training in counterinsurgency, counter-terror, and the establishment of "irregular forces" began in the early 1960s (McClintock, 1985:62). According to McClintock, U.S. theories of counterinsurgency, elaborated at the U.S. Army School of Special Warfare at Fort Bragg, were exported to Guatemala just after the emergence of an armed insurgency. Expanding these doctrines, Guatemala adopted tactical measures of population control that had been used in other countries and took some of the prescriptions of counterinsurgency theory to extremes by creating model villages and the civil patrol system.

Guatemala's version of counterinsurgency was also strongly influenced by the experiences of military institutions in other Latin American countries. Latin American military institutions are, for the most part, constitutionally defined as apolitical or non-partisan servants of ideal national interests that transcend partisan affiliation. Thus Latin American military regimes saw themselves–because of their functional loyalty to national interests construed as superseding the banality of everyday politics–as the only viable option left to further the social and economic development of their countries. Many of Latin America's 20th century military regimes sought to modernize and promote their visions of the nation by ruling through the elimination of dissent. According to Loveman and Davis (1989), Latin American military regimes believed that they were especially equipped to determine the destiny and character of their nation:

> Patriotism, nationalism, self-sacrifice, and absolute commitment to the national welfare and security distinguished military officers, in their own opinion, from the self-seeking, venal civilian politicians, who served special interests rather than those of the nation. The perfection of antipolitics required non-political leadership. (Loveman, 1989:7)

The antipolitical stance of Latin American military thought and the rise to power of authoritarian military regimes was compounded by U.S. policies that were centred in the belief that military institutions throughout the region must be bolstered so that they might act to hold back the threat of communist insurgency (Loveman, 1989:9,174). The combination of an inherently authoritarian and messianic Latin American military logic with the logistical and financial backing from the United States abetted the formation of highly militarized societies in a number of Latin American countries that relied heavily on state-sponsored violence and the logic of anticommunism (O'Brien, 1985).

In Guatemala, modern counterinsurgency strategies were established with U.S. aid in the mid-1960s, shortly after the emergence of the first generation of Guatemalan insurgent groups. The first generation of counterinsurgency strategies was based on National Security doctrine that, according to its intellectual author–General Hector Gramajo Morales, was brought into play as a result of the U.S training in military operations that Guatemalan Armed Forces personnel received beginning in 1954 (Gramajo Morales, 1995:99). As outlined in the Guatemalan Armed Forces' National Stability Thesis, the objectives deemed to be in the interest of national security were to be achieved, by eliminating all obstacles, through the use of "political, economic, psychosocial, and military actions" (1988:7). Thus, counterinsurgency policies were part of an arsenal designed not primarily to limit insurgency but to re-structure the Guatemalan nation to fit the image held to be in the best interests of the armed forces.[1]

The information drawn from espionage, infiltration, the tapping of state-collected citizen information archives, surveillance, and torture made possible the Guatemalan Armed Forces' military counterinsurgency operations that included massacres, extra-judicial assassinations, disappearances, tortures, and the establishment of strictly controlled military zones. In general, intelligence collection in Guatemala was co-ordinated through the Ministry of National Defence.[2]

Though intelligence gathering is a key element of effective counter-insurgency administration, the power of the intelligence gathering apparatus over civilians is reflective of the subjective way in which it is collected, combined with the selective application of extra-judicial military justice (Schirmer, 1999:255). As a result, the power of intelligence specialists was not just due to their privileged access to information but also due to their ability to label ordinary citizens as insurgents; and their active participation in and organization of extra-judicial forms of military justice such as torture, disappearances, assassinations, and raids.[3]

Counterinsurgency in Guatemala was not limited to the efficient collection of intelligence and its corollary application of iniquitous forms of military justice. Using the entrenched counterinsurgency method of establishing periods of "legal exception" that could allow for greater room for the military to manoeuvre, the Guatemalan Armed Forces attempted to legalize not only their political and economic program of social re-structuring but also the application of iniquitous forms of military justice. Though their success in the legalization of anti-insurgent extra-judicial assassinations was short lived, the military governments during *La Violencia* were able to effectively use the periods of legal exception to gain full control of the state apparatus and to play an active role in the re-design of Guatemala's constitution.

The application of iniquitous and arbitrary executions, disappearances, and torture also allowed the counterinsurgency apparatus to "ideologically" influence its target population through terror. The exertion of "ideological" influence, defined in military terms as a psychological operation, is generally analyzed in relation to the armed forces' use of propaganda and misinformation. In terms of propaganda, armed forces personnel were involved in the active denial of involvement in human rights abuses wherever plausible, control of the media, and in the establishment of rural development programmes.[4] Yet the Guatemalan military's arsenal of tools used in psychological operations went far beyond simple propaganda and misinformation. The success of the Guatemalan Armed Forces' psychological operations lays in their ability to integrate elements of *ladinos'* vision of Guatemalan society and character into advertisements that promoted anticommunism and naturalized the paternal role of the military.[5]

COUNTERINSURGENCY POLICIES IN PRACTICE

This section addresses how the practice of counterinsurgency policies heightened gender and ethnic inequalities already present in Guatemalan society prior to *La Violencia*. Counterinsurgency policies targeting the primarily indigenous countryside focused on radically reconstructing indigenous culture and society. In addition to the use of invasive and destructive military strategies, the Guatemalan Armed Forces promoted an alternative religious affiliation meant to draw indigenous peoples in to the social order that the military's national order envisioned. The Armed Force's vision of the new counterinsurgent nation and state required the near destruction of certain forms of indigenous culture and the physical annihilation of many indigenous communities. In essence, the Armed Force's vision of the Guatemalan nation favoured the historical primacy of *ladino* Guatemalan society.

Nevertheless, the Guatemalan Armed Forces did not stop at targeting and restucturing indigenous society alone. They also sought to shape *ladino* society and culture for their own interests. This section will also show how the Guatemalan military used established *ladino* gender norms and how they capitalized on women's images to further a discriminatory construction of *ladino* women in need of paternal control and surveillance.

Indigenous Peoples as Counterinsurgency Targets

The application of counterinsurgency policies in Guatemala was perhaps most creative during the holding stage of counterinsurgency programmes. The rural "development" programmes promoted by the armed forces' civilian affairs branch (S-5) within the context of counterinsurgency were meant to "win the hearts of the Mayan people" and to improve the image of the armed forces abroad and at home. Implemented primarily in rural areas that were believed to have the potential for guerrilla activity, holding strategies such as model villages, food for work programmes, and civil patrols were used so as to limit the potential development of future guerrilla activity. The complexities of the long-term effects of these programmes have been documented in a number of recent ethnographic studies (Green, 1999; Perera, 1993; Carmack, 1988). These studies suggest that counterinsurgency programmes acted to radically restructure Guatemalan cultural life for both indigenous peoples and for the national elites.

Carol Smith's "The Destruction of the Material Bases of Indian Culture" provides insight into the varied and potentially long-term economic impacts of violent counterinsurgency strategies (Smith, 1988:206). Smith explores the case of Totonicapan where the violence of the 1980s did not materialize in the form of death and torture, but in the virtual destruction of the integrated regional economy from which most of the towns people of San Miguel, Totonicapan made a living. In San Miguel, townspeople earned income by making and trading artisanal goods that had, until then, been traded in "a well developed Indian market economy" that allowed for the self-sufficiency of the town's artisans (Smith, 1988:215).

The destruction of the Indian market economy was a result of scorched earth counterinsurgency policies that ostensibly sought to eradicate guerrilla organizations by wiping out entire indigenous communities in the Guatemalan highlands. The obliteration of more than 400 indigenous villages in the first part of the 1980s had as its goal the removal of any potential food or shelter source for guerrilla groups hiding in highland jungles. Yet, scorched earth policies–the obliteration of indigenous communities and their food supply through massacres and the systematic burning of subsistence crops–had a devastating impact on rural indigenous Guatemalans and brought about the displacement of nearly two million people from the country-side (REMHI, 1999). The flight of rural Guatemalans into refugee camps in Mexico, into the cities' shanty towns, and into hiding in the jungle put together with the outright obliteration of indigenous communities had far-reaching consequences, including reducing the demand for artisan goods manufactured in towns not directly affected by violence.

From a local perspective, Smith noted an increased participation of townspeople in seasonal plantation work, greater migration of San Migueleños to larger towns and cities, and a marked downturn in the future expectations of formerly affluent artisans (Smith, 1988:215). The explanation of these local phenomena led Smith to an assessment of the region's economic situation resulting from national counterinsurgency policies. Counterinsurgency actions prior to 1982 had left room for the existence of an integrated regional indigenous market network in the highlands because of the selective (mainly urban) targets that earlier military governments had favoured. By contrast counterinsurgency policies that began in the early 1980s changed this system forever, consciously targeting not only those communities that were physically destroyed by the army or by the cross-fires of the civil war but also by attempting to destroy what Smith has defined as the bases for the survival of indigenous culture in the whole of highland Guatemala: the autonomous community (Smith, 1988:230). The macro-economic indicators for the post-1982 period, discussed in section 4, substantiate Smith's local findings.

Psychological counterinsurgency operations also targeted indigenous communities with the intention of permanently altering their cultural fabric. Ríos Montt's near fanatical adhesion to evangelical Protestant ideals is perhaps the most blatant example of discourse that links the moral, religious, and nationalist dimension of counterinsurgency policies. Ríos Montt, born-again into the Christian evangelical Church of the Word (*El Verbo*),[6] openly used Christian evangelical doctrine in his attempt to re-structure Guatemalan society between 1982 and 1983. In order to finance the militarized re-structuring of the countryside, Ríos Montt relied on the fundraising efforts of the Summer Institute of Linguistics and Wycliffe Bible Translators as well as those of Love Lift International (Gospel Outreach Relief) (Perera, 1993:88).

Ríos Montt's messianic vision of Guatemala became a *cause célèbre* within U.S. Christian fundamentalist circles and earned him the financial support of prominent figures like Jack Kemp and Pat Robertson. In addition to financial support, Christian fundamentalist leaders supported Ríos Montt's propaganda efforts abroad by promoting him as a deeply moral figure in charge of a corrupt military engaged in a war with Christian nemeses (Anfuso, 1984). As a result, Ríos Montt was able to garner substantial financial support at a time when direct bilateral aid from the U.S. had been reduced because of Guatemala's international image as a human rights violator.

The effects of Ríos Montt's promotion of evangelical Protestant groups within the counterinsurgency plan was socially significant because it resulted in the "conversion" of approximately a third of primarily rural indigenous Guatemalans from syncretic forms of Catholicism to evangelical Protestantism by the end of *La Violencia* (Perera, 1993:89,330; Green, 1999:150). Though evangelical Protestant missions had been in Guatemala since the 19th century, it was not until the 1980s that indigenous Guatemalans turned to evangelical Protestantism as a way to safeguard their lives in conflict zones (Green, 1999:152-153).

Ríos Montt and his supporters saw that drawing indigenous peoples away from Liberation Theology-inspired Catholic movements would be an ideological victory that would ensure that left-leaning armed insurgents would not be able to find receptive minds in the countryside. Other factions within the Guatemalan Armed Forces–though in agreement with the need to reframe the minds of potential insurgents–saw

Ríos Montt's evangelical messianism as a threat to their position within Guatemala's economic and political hierarchy (Perera, 1993:331).

Nevertheless even after Ríos Montt's overthrow in 1983, Mejia Victores continued to link the inculcation of Christian morality with the development of a peaceful nation, invoking the help of God in the task of re-building the nation. The belief in God and the promotion of family values are key to military discourses of counterinsurgency–both prior to and post-Ríos Montt–because the threat of armed insurgency is described not in military terms but rather as a threat to the values that stand at the core of what the military presented as the essential Guatemalan character. Engaged in fratricidal state-sponsored violence, the military sought to reframe anticommunist and anti-insurgent discourse to fit within the scope of its mandate. The defence of the nation was, after all, the role for which the armed forces were founded.

Targeting the Ladino Woman and the Construction of a Guatemalan Nation

Counterinsurgency policies also used *ladino* female bodies and carefully constructed images of women and the family to express their ideals of a nation. Guatemalan military governments during the height of the civil war (1978-1984) made effective use of the print media in order to promote counterinsurgency messages and to publicly demonstrate the consequences of dissent. During the height of Guatemala's civil war, tortured and violated female bodies or cadavers were displayed in daily newspapers alongside "Wanted" posters representing innocent-looking young women explicitly defined as dangerous guerrillas-on-the-run. For the purposes of constructing an image of the ideal counterinsurgent Guatemalan nation, women–and in particular women who transgressed traditional values–had to be tamed and displayed through violence.

During *La Violencia*, women were neither killed nor tortured as often as men. Nevertheless, when women were victims of political violence, the type of violation to which they were subjected is closely tied to their gender. The Commission for Historical Clarification (CEH) estimates that only twenty-five percent of all victims of violence whose sex is known were women (CEH, 1999). According to the statistical analysis of Guatemala's institutionalized violence made by Ball, Krobark and Spirer, at the beginning of *La Violencia* (1978-81), women were between 5-10 percent of the violence victims (1999:88). During Ríos Montt's term in office, and particularly at the height of the scorched earth policies aimed primarily at indigenous populations, the percentage of women as victims of state-sponsored violence rose to between 15-25 percent (Ball, 1999:89).

In stark contrast to their under-representation as murder and torture victims, *Memory of Silence* points out that women were vastly over-represented in sexual crimes making up 99 percent of the total figure (CEH, 1999:19). REMHI states that the rape of women was a systematic practice for Guatemalan military operatives and used both as a training tool for recruits as well as a "morale booster" for operatives working in the field (1999a:212).

Keeping in mind the particularities of how women fared within overall statistics of violence in Guatemala is not only important because it may remind the reader that women were not the preferred or usual targets of the armed forces' military operations. Keeping the statistical context in mind also allows the reader to see how, because of their distinctiveness, women's bodies and images–when displayed in newspapers–do gain significant symbolic power and importance in the armed forces' psychological counterinsurgency operations.

Although political violence is gendered in its execution, political violence's gendering in Guatemala is best seen in the way that the Guatemalan Armed Forces chose to display its targets. Counterinsurgency advertisement, though not limited to the display of female images, made use of women's bodies and images so as to promote a cohesive image of a "moral" counterinsurgent nation. In constructing a sense of national "morality," the Guatemalan Armed Forces built on culturally established gender roles and images by capitalizing on an image of women guerrillas as the utmost transgressor of the natural order.

During Ríos Montt's term in office, the most blatant forms of counterinsurgency advertisements appeared in a series that I have titled "Turn Them In," or in the more literal translation "Denounce Them." As demonstrated by the excerpts, these full-page advertisements appear just after the issuing of the first set of amnesty decrees of the early 1980s.[7] They feature an individual's name and picture as the most prominent elements of the composition. The second most prominent items are the individual's supposed guerrilla affiliation (using only the abbreviations of the organization's names) and the ad-ending slogan "CSN-National Security Council. Maintaining peace is also your business."

The message in these ads is simple: the individuals featured, both men and women, are described as "enemies" or "dangers" to both the Guatemalan individual and his family and to the nation as a whole, and readers are urged to turn these individuals into the authorities. What is unsettling to the viewer of this series is the youth and innocence of the pictures featured as well as the inordinate number of young women shown as threats. Marta Regina Töck, seen in the excerpt that follows, is a fitting example:

> Marta Regina Töck. Member of ORPA [Armed People's Organization]
>
> Marta Regina Töck also known by the alias "MARIA JOSE", abandoned university to join ORPA, a communist organization that aims to destroy Guatemala through crime and terror . . .
>
> Marta Regina Töck rejected the opportunity that amnesty afforded her in June of the current year. If you help us find her, we may yet be able to avoid her continuation of her unpatriotic [anti-national] war. Denounce her because she is also a danger to you and your family. (Excerpted from *Prensa Libre*, 8 November 1982:S16)

The ads present a short story detailing the type of crime in which the individual is involved, their proven rejection of society, the foreign training or ties of each individual, and often a vignette that shows how she/he became involved in subversion.

These stories describe fallen innocence and tarnished potential. They all show relatively young people on their way to becoming respected professionals and who because of their confused idealism and/or because of some foreign pressure, in the form of influential literature or un-described forces, become involved in the destruction of themselves and their country. All individuals are described as threats to the country and its way of life because of their purported involvement in terrorism and crime. In Marta's case, she is portrayed contiguously as an individual in need of rescuing and as a threat. The threat factor is spelled out further in the ad featuring another young woman, Lidia Amparo Santos:

> Lidia Amparo Santos Chacón, alias "Yali" or "Julia", is a young Guatemalan teacher who in her attempts to change Guatemala, chose the extremist path of terror and violence without realizing that in doing so, she became an instrument of interests foreign to the authentic destiny of our country.
>
> Lidia Amparo Santos Chacón took advantage of her work as a teacher for the "Casa Central" school in Guatemala City by involving immature young women, and attaining their enrollment in

the subversive activities of the extremist communist group called ORPA.

Because of her subversive and extreme acts, Lidia Amparo Santos Chacón, alias "Yali" or "Julia", is a danger to you and your loved ones. (Excerpted from *Prensa Libre*, 6 December 1982:25)

Lidia is a risk because of her naiveté, her proximity to other impressionable youths, and because of her participation in undefined "extreme acts." Unlike Marta Regina Töck, Lidia is constructed as being beyond salvation. One gets the sense that it isn't only her youth to which the authors link her confusion; her gender is also alluded to as the culprit. In this story's first paragraph she is not an agent but a vessel used by foreign interests to entice other young women by taking advantage of the role of teacher—a position of high esteem that she originally held in Guatemalan society. The fall from a position of privilege to the role of a criminal/terrorist with a known alias is a common motif in this series of ads. In their fall from grace through their engagement in activities defined as terrorist, the youths are depicted as not only violating the law but more importantly as betraying their nation.

Yet, who were the target audience for this type of publicity? If we follow traditional advertising protocol it is most likely that these ads targeted similarly "well-intentioned" young men and women and that they thus aimed to demonstrate to them the dangers of socially-inclined activism. Additionally, however, I would suggest that these ads were intended for the public in general, as warnings concerning the girl- or boy-next-door type of criminal to look out for. As a series, these ads demand the vigilance and the involvement of all readers in ending insurgency. The ads force parents to look at their youths' activities in a new light and they force youths to be cautious as to who they associate with and about the causes that they might be involved in. Because the ads show how these fallen heroes fell, they strongly suggest to all readers a safe course of action and safe rationale for being Guatemalan.

Finally, because of the over-representation of women in these ads, I would also suggest that they were meant to suggest surveillance of women in particular. Diane Nelson's work on gender and ethnicity shows how women who are seen as transgressing the accepted norms of behaviour are constantly scrutinized and publicly disciplined (Nelson, 1999:171). Furthermore, Nelson's work suggests that images of women, indigenous and non-indigenous, have traditionally been used in Guatemala to construct national identities (Nelson, 1999). The use of the image of the transgressing guerrilla woman was fitting for counterinsurgency purposes because it reinforced a culturally established norm of constructing national identities through the surveillance and discipline of women who were perceived as the fundamental yet vulnerable core of the nation.

Green's (1999) account of the devastating impact of rape by Guatemalan Armed Forces personnel on contemporary indigenous communities is a blunt reminder of the brutal mechanisms through which the surveillance and punishment of women changed individuals and the society as a whole. The use of rape as part of the practice of massacres in the countryside created a lasting legacy of fear, social disintegration, and systemic distrust not only for the individual women affected but also more generally for their communities (Green, 1999). Thus, the taming and disciplining of women was not solely left in the domain of advertising or national image-making but was part and parcel of the everyday practice of counterinsurgency.

ECONOMIC IMPACT OF COUNTERINSURGENCY POLICIES

Military counterinsurgency strategies, particularly those developed beginning in 1982, were designed to have economic benefits for different elites. The military's management of the Guatemalan economy and its relationship to the primary economic elites affected the development of counterinsurgency policies. As the Military Junta's Current National Objectives for 1982 indicate, the military's counterinsurgency project aimed to:

> achieve a national economic recuperation through the free-market system . . . To encourage the intensification, within the ranks of the economic pressure groups a new developmentalist, reformist, and nationalist way of thinking (Gramajo Morales, 1995:180).

Yet the same objectives also offered an economic vision that could be perceived as a threat by Guatemalan economic elites since the Military Junta sought to "improve the quality of life of the population so as to diminish the existing contradictions of the country" (Gramajo Morales, 1995:180).

This section is a brief outline of Guatemala's economic situation during *La Violencia* and highlights the macro-economic changes apparent during this period. The presentation of the country's economic portrait will be followed by an analysis of the changing relationship between the military elites and economic elites throughout the period of *La Violencia*. To conclude, this section will explore the economic benefits that military elites derived from their active pursuit of counterinsurgency strategies.

I argue that because the military's counterinsurgency plans formed part of an economic as well as a political project, the role of the Guatemalan economy and the country's economic elites in the development and later curtailment of overtly violent counterinsurgency strategies should not be underrated. Particularly at the beginning of *La Violencia,* the Guatemalan military received extensive support from various sectors of the economic elites in order to develop its counterinsurgency plans. In the early stages of the implementation of counterinsurgency strategies, Guatemalan economic elites were reluctant to oppose counterinsurgency practices because they enjoyed virtually uncontested economic control over Central America's strongest economy. Because insurgents were billed primarily as promoting an anti-capitalist agenda that could threaten their privileged position, economic elites turned at least a blind eye to the increasingly violent tactics of the military, and at worst funded and used military personnel and policies to further their own ends. As counterinsurgency plans furthered the economic position of the Guatemalan military establishment, the relationship between the economic elites and the military came under increasing strain. Military elites began to gradually entrench themselves into the national economic landscape as their share of the country's business and development opportunities grew through their privileged position as the sole safeguard against the threat of insurgency and terrorism.

The Economy and Counterinsurgency

The instability caused by political violence combined with the general slowdown of the global economy in the late 1970s and early 1980s had long-lasting negative effects on the Guatemalan economy. Between 1970 and 1980 the Guatemalan economy grew at an average rate of 5.7% per year. Between 1980-81, however, the Guatemalan economy was contracting at a rate of 3.5% per year. On average, between 1980 and 1985 the Guatemalan economy contracted at a rate of 1.4% per year. Contraction or minimal growth (0.6% or less) characterized the Guatemalan economy until 1986-87 when it began to make gains by growing at a rate of 3.6%. Although at the beginning of the global crisis Guatemala could still boast respectable GDP growth, the country's economy took an inordinately long time to recover from the global downturn. It took nearly a decade for the Guatemalan economy to again reach the levels of expansion seen in the late 1970s.

Despite the generalized economic slowdown that Guatemala was experiencing, up to the late 1970s the country could still be considered to have the strongest of the Central American economies (*Inforpress*, December 14th, 1981:3). In 1980, Guatemala had a relatively good rate of GDP growth (4%), the lowest rate of inflation in Central America (10.9%), and one of the lowest amounts of public sector debt ($950 million US dollars) (monies owed to both domestic and foreign sources).[8] By the mid 1980s, however, Guatemala's economic conditions had worsened, making its performance poor even by Central American standards.

The reduced economic well-being of Guatemalans *vis-à-vis* other Central Americans was a long term effect of the economic downturn that peaked during the height of *La Violencia*. In 1998, according to World Bank estimates, 53% of the Guatemalan population lived in poverty (earning under one US dollar per day)–a figure that is higher than the rates of poverty estimated for Costa Rica (18.9%), Honduras (46.9%), and Nicaragua (43.8%) (InfoGroup, 1999:251). In terms of the United Nations' Human Development Index, Guatemala ranked below Costa Rica, El Salvador, and Honduras even ten years after the end of *La Violencia* (InfoGroup, 1999:251). By the time of the signing of the Guatemalan Peace Accords in 1996, the population was still suffering the consequences of counterinsurgency-aided underdevelopment. In 1996, Guatemala's illiteracy rate was 40%, some 35% of Guatemalans did not have access to potable water, and over 40% of the population was deemed to have seriously restricted access to health services (InfoGroup, 1999).

The contraction in the Guatemalan economy can be seen to be in part a result of the effects of political violence. Rural-centred counterinsurgency policies resulted in extremely high chronic unemployment and underemployment rates ranging from 49% in 1985 to–at their lowest since *La Violencia*–46% in 1998 (InfoGroup, 1999:69). Adding to the demand-constraining effects of high unemployment rates, inflation rates following *La Violencia* were unusually high, reaching a level of 35% in 1985. To make matters worse, the uncertainty that resulted from the high-levels of political violence resulted in both a reduction in investment levels and internal demand (due to plummeting real incomes). While the Guatemalan economy contracted and unemployment increased, the country's external debt grew exponentially, to 2,472 million US dollars by 1985.

While in 1977 Guatemala's foreign debt was already 176.5 million US dollars, by 1980 the country's foreign debt had risen to 570 million US dollars (*Inforpress*, December 14th, 1981:3). During the late 1970s and early 1980s, Guatemala acquired increasing levels of foreign debt while also experiencing a drop in its international monetary reserves. In 1980 alone, Guatemala suffered a drop of 251 million US dollars in its international monetary reserve fund (*Inforpress*, December 14th, 1981:3). As Rachel McCleary explains, the military governments of the 1970s were engaged in financing import substitution strategies and enlarging the public sector through the use of readily available foreign financing (McCleary, 1999:49).

The Guatemalan military's mismanagement of Guatemala's economy is due, in part, to overspending on defence. Spending on defence during General Lucas Garcia's (1978-1982) term in office grew at an average of 14% per year, with the highest levels of spending in his last full year (1981). During both Ríos Montt and Mejia Victores' terms in office (1982-1984), the rate of growth of spending on defence dropped to approximately 1.5% per year (Scheetz, 1996:2). While this 1.5% increase in military expenditure may seem conservative, it is important to note that during 1982-1984 Guatemala was experiencing a substantial contraction of its economy (*Inforpress*, July 31st, 1981:2). As a result–even though the military increased its defence spending only minimally–in 1984 the defence budget used upwards of 30 percent of the government's taxation income (Scheetz, 1996).

Yet changes in expenditure in defense are not enough to indicate the national impact of an over-emphasis on military and security spending. Even though the total monies spent on defence grew at lower rates during the Ríos Montt and Mejia Victores periods than in Lucas Garcia's term in office, during the early to mid-1980s the defence budget grew to encompass 22.1% of the total government spending compared to the 13.9% share assigned to defence by Lucas Garcia's government (Scheetz, 1996:4).

It is possible to view the military's overemphasis on spending as a cost not only to the general population but also to the profit margin of the traditional Guatemalan economic elite. The way that the economy was managed during *La Violencia* might have been part of a concerted effort on the part of the Guatemalan military as an institution to cement its position as both a political and economic elite. The institution continued to increase the public budget devoted to the military sector and ensured that the salaries of military personnel were raised well beyond those of other public sector workers.

Economic Benefits of Counterinsurgency

The question of whether or not the Guatemalan military or its members gained economic benefits from their involvement in counterinsurgency can be answered in different ways. One could look at possible direct profits derived from counterinsurgency policies. This approach could include the examination of the short- or long-term economic benefits of and/or goods expropriated during the civil war for the institution as a whole or the forces' individual members; it could also include an assessment of whether or not the institution or its individual members used more than their share of public funds for the simple purpose of enriching their own coffers.

A number of authors have suggested that the Guatemalan Armed Forces as an institution did gain influence as a result of the increased concentration of resources and administrative functions that fell under their control as part of the requirements of national security. By 1985, for instance, the Guatemalan Armed Forces had effective control over Guatemala's national military and civilian airlines, the international airport authority, Guatemala's national telephone company (GUATEL), a television station (Channel 5), factories producing military supplies, and a national bank (*Banco del Ejército*) (Delli Sante, 1996:31; Perera, 1993:54).

As for administrative functions that can be construed to have had substantial economic spin-offs, counterinsurgency policies carried out by the Guatemalan Armed Forces placed the institution in control of the social and economic restructuring of the countryside that had been decimated during the "civil war." These functions included the relocation and reconstruction of rural settlements, the provision of health, transportation, education, and religious services, and the disbursement of foreign aid (Delli Sante, 1996:32). Looking at the potential institutional gains to the Guatemalan military of its control of national businesses or key administrative functions, however, does not take into account the uneven distribution of resources within the ranks of the armed forces.

Other sources have suggested that particular military officers took advantage of their positions within the Guatemalan Armed Forces to enrich themselves through the sometimes forced acquisition of prime arable land from civilian and public sources, their control of important trade gateways, industrial monopolies, tax evasion, and/or through cor-

state-sponsored violence were deprived of their most basic rights while citizens defined as 'noninsurgents' were afforded full legal protections. The separation of Guatemalan society into 'insurgents,' 'probable insurgents,' 'potential insurgents,' and those explicitly defined as not involved in insurgency by the state apparatus could not help but create an unequal distribution of power.

In the long term, counterinsurgency violence furthered social inequality because the changes in the position of the Guatemalan Armed Forces into the country's economic and political elite, the effects of overemphasizing spending on military and under-spending in social services, and the effects that the legacy of fear left on the fabric of Guatemalan society. At the same time that the Guatemalan Armed Forces secured their position within Guatemalan elites through the practice of counterinsurgency, the climate of fear established by political violence ensured few would dare to question the ascent of the armed forces and their members into positions of political and economic power.

The Guatemalan military built their nationalistic rhetoric on accepted social inequalities, in part, because their purported defence of a seemingly commonsense vision of the Guatemalan nation allowed them to justify and naturalize the use of political violence against those who were labelled insurgents. Re-shaping Guatemalan society through targeting indigenous culture and furthering discriminatory gender constructions allowed the Guatemalan Armed Forces to create the image of a Guatemalan nation and state that best suited the rise and entrenchment of the military elite.

As discussed earlier, the reliance on an image of women in need of surveillance and discipline served the interest of a military regime intent on portraying itself as a paternal protector of true Guatemalaness. This symbolic positioning of the Guatemalan Armed Forces as the father of the nation allowed them to justify their arbitrary use of force as actions in the defence of the national character. At the same time, however, the Guatemalan Armed Forces' father-figure position rested on an unequal social positioning of women that, as Green (1999) and Nelson (1999) have shown, furthered pre-existing trends of discrimination. Thus, the furtherance of social inequality was not only a result of the acquisition of wealth by the military sector, but it was also a result of the fact that the military ensured that its social and economic restructuring of Guatemalan society rested on pre-existing social trends. The reliance of counterinsurgency policies on existing social inequalities served to ensure that its plan for social, political, and economic restructuring met with only minimal effective dissent.

NOTES

1. According to Gramajo Morales, the Guatemalan Armed Forces outlined a five phase plan for the development of counterinsurgency: (1) the pacification or clearing campaign known as *"Victoria 82"* or "Operation Ashes", under whose purview lay the obliteration of indigenous villages; (2) *"Firmeza* [Resolve] 83", a holding strategy through which civil patrols were introduced in the countryside; (3) *"Reencuentro Institucional* [Institutional Re-encounter] 84", another element of a holding strategy which envisioned the restructuring of society through model villages and the reinstatement of a constitutional process; (4) *"Estabilidad Nacional* [National Stability] 85", a holding strategy that promoted counterinsurgency through the extension of state structures into the countryside and the establishment of an armed forces monitoring of political life; and *"Avance* [Advancement] 86" which, according to Gramajo Morales, signalled the withdrawal of the Armed Forces from the everyday practice of politics (Schirmer, 1999).

2. Both specialized and non-specialized agents of the National Police, the Ambulatory Military Police, Military Commissioners, Military Reservists, Civil Patrols, and the infamous *Archivo* (under the direction of the Presidential General Staff) collected information. The Presidential General Staff (*Estado Mayor Presidencial*) will be henceforth abbreviated as EMP. This intelligence gathering body specialized in high-tech espionage in addition to its infamous reputation as a torture centre. According to Schirmer, there were four key organizations involved in intelligence gathering: the military intelligence directorate (D-2) which responded to the National Defence Chief of Staff; military security services (S-2) under the direction of military zone chiefs; special patrol groups (G-2); and the aforementioned *Archivo* (1998:254). All in all, Schirmer estimates that there were close to one thousand operatives involved in intelligence collection, either through the regular military ranks (D-2, S-2, and G-2), colloquially termed *La Regional*, or through the EMP's *El Archivo* (1999:254). For its military operations counterinsurgency relied heavily on the collection of intelligence on its own citizens and established citizen registries in order to further a comprehensive intelligence analysis apparatus. Intelligence was also gathered through the computerized survey of energy use patterns, telephone tapping, computerized cross-referenced population registries, infiltrated informants in guerrilla and popular organizations, and through the fruits of torture (REHMI, 1998). Yet, as suggested above, the activities of the intelligence gathering specialists within the military and the EMP did not constitute the full breath of the armed forces' intelligence gathering arsenal, as civil patrol members and civilian affairs military personnel (S-5) also collected and relayed intelligence.

3. Extra-judicial "justice" was not the exclusive purview of intelligence specialists. Paramilitary or irregular forces with unofficial links to the Guatemalan armed forces, police or EMP enabled the operation of a flexible counterinsurgency program that would allow military spokespersons to deny any involvement in the application of extra-judicial justice, wherever plausible. The role of unofficial forces in the selective assassinations that were required by Guatemala's counterinsurgency program was envisioned from the outset and began operating in different forms as early as the mid-1960s (REHMI, 1998).

4. See "Noticias Prohibidas" in *Prensa Libre,* July 7 1982:4.

5. The term *ladino* is specific to Guatemala and can mean individuals of mixed Indigenous and Spanish heritage. In most cases, the term is used to denote the "cultural" practices of the non-indigenous natives of the country.

6. The Church of the Word is a derivative of the Christian fundamentalist Gospel Outreach Movement based in California. The doctrines of the Church of the Word are explicitly anticommunist (Perera, 1993:88).

7. On the 27th of May 1982, law decree 33-82 gave amnesty for all crimes that resulted from an association with a subversive group and in those involved in crimes as a result of counterinsurgency activities, so long as individuals signed a declaration stating the nature of their past crimes and renounced insurgency. Ríos Montt's government extended amnesty again starting in March 1983, beginning with law decree 27-83.

8. In 1980, El Salvador's economy was contracting at a rate of 8.7% while the economies of Honduras and Costa Rica were experiencing modest growth rates of 2% and 1.9%, respectively. In terms of inflation, El Salvador (17.4%), Honduras (18.7%), and Costa Rica (18.1) experienced much higher rates of inflation (*Inforpress*, December 14th, 1981:3).

9. For instance, Colonel Juan Valencia (*Safari Seguridad*) and General Edgar Agusto Godoy Gaitán (*Metropol 2000*) have both been part of Guatemala's secret intelligence gathering systems (*El Archivo* [1991-3], and the integrated persons registry respectively) and been accused, among other things, of planning the murder of anthropologist Myrna Mack (*El Periodico*, April 3rd, 2000:3-4). Colonel Francisco Ortega Menaldo (also instrumental in the development of *Metropol 2000*) was head of military intelligence for Lucas Garcia (1978-1982) and former commander of military zone 13 and has been accused of participating, planning, and ordering extra-judicial executions (*El Periodico*, April 3rd, 2000:4).

REFERENCES

Anfuso, J., & Sczepanski, D. (1984). *Efrain Rios Montt: Servant or Dictator? The Real Story of Guatemala's Controversial Born-again President*. Ventura: Vision House.

Brenes, A. (1998). *Soldados como Empresarios: Los Negocios de los Militares en Centro America*. [Web Article]. Fundación Arias (Centro de Paz y Reconciliación). Retrieved September 20th, 2001, from the World Wide Web: *www.arias.or.cr/documentos/cpr/soldados.htm*

Carmack, R. (Ed.). (1988). *Harvest of Violence: The Mayan Indians and the Guatemalan Crisis*. Norman: University of Oklahoma Press.

Delli Sante, A. (1996). *Nightmare or Reality: Guatemala in the 1980s*. (Vol. 5). Amsterdam: Thela Publishers.

Gramajo Morales, H. A. (1995). *De la Guerra a la Guerra: La Difícil Transición Política en Guatemala*. Guatemala City: Fondo de Cultura Editorial.

Green, L. (1999). *Fear as a Way of Life: Mayan Widows in Rural Guatemala*. New York: Columbia University Press.

InfoGroup, G. (1999). *En Cifras: Guatemala: Perfil Integral del País* (Volume I, Number 1.1). Guatemala: Global InfoGroup.

Loveman, B., & Davies, T. M. (Eds.). (1989). *The Politics of Antipolitics: The Military in Latin America* (Second ed.). Lincoln: University of Nebraska Press.

Marchak, P. (1999). *God's Assassins: State Terrorism in Argentina in the 1970s*. Montreal: McGill-Queen's University Press.

McCleary, R. M. (1999). *Dictating Democracy: Guatemala and the End of Violent Revolution*. Gainesville: University of Florida Press.

McClintock, M. (1985). *The American Connection: Volume II-State Terror and Popular Resistance in Guatemala*. London: Zed Books.

Mora, F. O., & Wiktorowicz, Q. (2003). *Economic Reform and the Military: China, Cuba and Syria in Comparitive Perspective*. Paper presented at the Latin American Studies Association: The Global and the Local: Rethinking Area Studies, Dallas, Texas.

Nelson, Diane. (1999). *A Finger in the Wound: Body Politic in Quincentennial Guatemala*. Berkeley: University of California Press.

O'Brien, P., & Cammack, P. (Eds.). (1985). *Generals in Retreat: The Crisis of Military Rule in Latin America*. Manchester: Manchester University Press.

Perera, V. (1993). *Unfinished Conquest: The Guatemalan Tragedy*. Berkeley: University of California Press.

Scheetz, T. (1996). *Gastos Militares en Guatemala: Su Impacto Fiscal y Macroeconomico, 1969-1995* [Web Article]. Fundación Arias-Centro de Paz y Reconciliación. Retrieved September 20th, 2001, from the World Wide Web: *www.arias.or.cr/documentos/cpr/guat.htm*

Schirmer, J. (1999). *Las Intimidades del Proyecto Poítico de los Militares en Guatemala*. Guatemala: FLACSO.

Mexico's Progresa Program (1997-2000): An Example of Neo-Liberal Poverty Alleviation Programs Concerned with Gender, Human Capital Development, Responsibility and Choice

Lucy Luccisano

SUMMARY. This paper examines Mexico's Program for Education, Health and Nutrition (Progresa), as an example of neo-liberal trends influencing poverty alleviation initiatives. The stated goal of the program was to break the intergenerational cycles of poverty. This end was to be achieved by investing in the basic capacities of the poor, particularly poor women and their children. Basic capacities were to be developed through cash transfers for improved nutrition, scholarships for children, and preventative health measures. The key concern of this paper, however, is to examine how cash transfers for human capital development are more than instruments of poverty reduction. Rather, cash transfers

Lucy Luccisano, PhD, is Assistant Professor, Department of Sociology, Wilfrid Laurier University, 75 University Avenue West, Waterloo, Ontario, Canada, N2L 3C5 (E-mail: lluccisa@wlu.ca).

The Canadian International Development Research Centre provided funding for this project. The author wishes to thank Mexican policy officials who gave generously of their time; special thanks to Paula Maurutto and Pino Esposito for reading various drafts of this article and making suggestions.

[Haworth co-indexing entry note]: "Mexico's Progresa Program (1997-2000): An Example of Neo-Liberal Poverty Alleviation Programs Concerned with Gender, Human Capital Development, Responsibility and Choice." Luccisano, Lucy. Co-published simultaneously in *Journal of Poverty* (The Haworth Press, Inc.) Vol. 8, No. 4, 2004, pp. 31-57; and: *Poverty and Inequality in the Latin American-U.S. Borderlands: Implication of U.S. Interventions* (ed: Keith M. Kilty, and Elizabeth A. Segal) The Haworth Press, Inc., 2004, pp. 31-57. Single or multiple copies of this article are available for a fee from The Haworth Document Delivery Service [1-800-HAWORTH, 9:00 a.m. - 5:00 p.m. (EST). E-mail address: docdelivery@haworthpress.com].

are also techniques that effect a new way of governing individual conduct. The intended effect of Progresa was a change in the subjectivity of
poor women from the passive recipients of aid to empowered market
subjects who were now given the freedom to make choices, albeit limited choices. However, subjects could now also be regulated through the
choices they make. The Progresa program can be said to represent a government through freedom, which in turn signals a shift from governing
through the direct administration of state institutions [read "passive"] to
that of governing through the "active" and responsible choices of individuals and their families. *[Article copies available for a fee from The
Haworth Document Delivery Service: 1-800-HAWORTH. E-mail address:
<docdelivery@haworthpress.com> Website: <http://www.HaworthPress.com>
© 2004 by The Haworth Press, Inc. All rights reserved.]*

KEYWORDS. Neo-liberal anti-poverty programs, gender, human capital development, cash transfer, and choice

Developments in anti-poverty programs in Latin America and Mexico from the 1990s to 2000 have been shaped by neo-liberal influences
arising from pressures from international financial institutions and national policy agendas. World Bank development reports and strategies
have influenced much of Latin American and Mexican anti-poverty
policies targeting human capital development. Neo-liberal anti-poverty
programs are designed to make the poor responsible for their own fu-
tures by instilling in them a sense of entrepreneurship. The objective is
to encourage the poor to pursue choices that will increase their opportunities and incomes. The values, assumptions and concepts behind the
new anti-poverty programs mark a shift in perception from the previously held notion of the poor as "children" needing to be rescued by the
interventionist [and paternalistic] state to the neo-liberal notion of the
poor as "adults" with rights, choices and responsibilities.

The new policy discourse has a progressive ring that deserves attention.
However, the logic underpinning such programs ignores the fundamental
features of Latin American and Mexican society and contemporary political economy that generate poverty. The intention of such anti-poverty programs is to "re-constitute" the poor as active, rational and responsible
individuals who are capable of managing their own problems without any
major redistribution of resources or shift in the neo-liberal economic strategy. In this way the new policy discourse is a two-edged sword. It makes

the poor feel more empowered to influence their own possible future success, but it also makes them feel more responsible for their current poverty and any possible failure to overcome this poverty in the future.

This article examines Mexico's Program for Education, Health and Nutrition (Progresa) as an example of patterns of poverty alleviation strategies in Latin America.[1] Ernesto Zedillo's signature Progresa program was launched on August 8th, 1997, mid-way into his presidential term. Households that qualified for the Progresa program received monthly medical attention, as well as cash transfers for food and children's education. The program was granted for a three-year period with possibilities for renewal. The program was designed to invest in the human capital development of poor women and their children. The Mexican government indicated that Progresa[2] was designed to be a future oriented program geared toward breaking the intergenerational, "vicious cycles of poverty" so that the extremely poor could lead virtuous lives (J. Goméz de León, personal communication, January 29, 1999).[3] The officially intended outcome of these strategies was the production of new subjectivities such as, the "rational and empowered women" [as they now managed the families' cash income], the "healthy and responsible mothers" [as they engaged in preventative health care] and "active parents" [as they monitored their children's educational performance].

Argued in this article is that anti-poverty programs like Progresa become popular because of the rhetoric of investing in human capital, but in reality, they are more about changing the subjectivity of the poor in order to more effectively govern them. In particular, they are aimed at influencing women to make "responsible" choices. In sum, discourses on investing in human capital are used to justify particular policy directions that include lean, cost-efficient and market-led economic development. The justification and the broader policy framework into which such programs are inserted have an indirect social regulation consequence.

GENDER AND ANTI-POVERTY PROGRAMS

Anti poverty programs like Progresa are, in part, a response to international pressure to address women's global economic inequality and poverty. For the last three decades, the international development apparatus, including the World Bank (WB) and the Inter-American Development Bank (IADB), has included women in their agenda for poverty alleviation and economic development. The 1990s, in particular, saw an increase in attention to women witnessed in the numerous international forums that addressed women's inequality. These included the UN world conferences in Cairo (International Conference on Population and Development, 1994), Copenhagen (World Summit for Social Development, 1995), Beijing (UN Fourth World Conference on Women, 1995), and New York (Beijing+5 June, 2000). At these international forums, women's organizations demanded that policies be implemented to respond to women's economic inequality and poverty by allowing them the opportunity to have sustainable livelihoods. In response to international pressures over the last three decades, international financial institutions and Latin American countries have designed various programs in the hopes of furthering poverty alleviation and economic development. Mexico's Progresa program represents one example of such efforts.

Scholars working in the area of gender, development and Latin American studies have written about the problematic inclusion of gender in poverty alleviation policies (Alvarez, 1996, 1998; Barrig, 1996, 1998; Blondet, 1995; Jelin, 1990; Lind, 1992, 1996, 1997; Luccisano, 2001; Rowlands, 1997; Schild, 1998, 2000a, 2000b, 2001; Townsend, 1999). With respect to anti-poverty programs, three important themes emerge from this literature. First, scholars have observed that spontaneous survival strategies adopted by poor women to deal with their social reproductive needs, such as feeding children and elders, have been institutionalized as inexpensive state welfare practices. That is, the government will provide some start-up funds for an anti-poverty program, but women must provide in-kind labor contribution. Mexican and Peruvian community kitchens are examples of the trends to institutionalize women's volunteerism (Barrig, 1996, 1998; Blondet, 1995; Luccisano, 2001). In these "community kitchens" the women received some funding and/or supplies, but they engaged in the administration of the kitchen, which included domestic tasks such as cooking, food shopping, and cleaning. Hence, the success of the program relied upon female volunteers carrying out a government nutrition program. This is one of the many examples of the trend toward uncontested gendered volunteerism as part of inexpensive government anti-poverty and welfare strategies.

Second, the politicized feminist concept of women's empowerment has been de-politicized and incorporated as part of international and state policy discourse. In the mid-seventies, third world feminists introduced the language of empowerment into the project of development. Empowerment was a term that conveyed the notion of challenging asymmetrical power relations between men and women. Moreover, the concept of empowerment, according to Savitri Bisnath and Diane Elson, was used to "frame and facilitate the struggle for social justice and women's equality through a transformation of economic, social and political structures at national and international levels" (2000). Recently, the concept of empowerment has lost its politicized meaning because it is being mobilized outside of a feminist agenda. Sonia Alvarez refers to this process as the "relatively rapid appropriation or absorption of some new and historic feminist ideas and issues by the mainstream of contemporary Latin American states and societies" (Alvarez cited in Townsend et al., 1999, p. 56). The de-politicized notion of empowerment appears in anti-poverty policies and World Bank documents. The term is strategic as it operates to individualize poverty. Moreover, Bisnath and Elson argue that the concept of empowerment as understood by the World Bank "is focused on enlarging the choices and productivity levels of individual women for the most part, in isolation from a feminist agenda, and in the context of a withdrawal of state responsibility for broad-based economic and social support" (2000). Therefore, the neo-liberal notion of empowerment means giving poor women the right to make choices within a context of dwindled state resources and few viable options.

Third, feminist scholarship cautions us to not understand all programs as completely closed spaces (Rowlands, 1997; Townsend et al., 1999). Feminist scholarship has cited examples which illustrate that some neo-liberal programs have become politicized experiences for some women. For example, some income-generating activities have allowed women to gain a degree of 'power over' their lives (Townsend et al., 1999). Other feminist scholars have noted that anti-poverty programs have also opened up spaces that produced unforeseen consequences such as political learning and activism (Jelin, 1991; Schild, 1998; Luccisano, 2001). While a form of liberation can be gained, old forms of control continue and new forms of domination arise. One of the key problems identified with anti-poverty programs in particular, and social development programs in general, is that strategic gender interests, such as the establishment of legal and social measures to ensure gender equality, the enactment for the passing of legislation on violence against women, and the attainment of reproductive rights, receive no attention.

The neo-liberal notion of empowerment and choice, with a subtext of gendered volunteerism, are key features of the Progresa program. Examined here is how empowerment, choice and freedom are understood as a productive form of power, which abandons more direct or disciplinary forms of power and operates through the choices that people make. In this context, cash transfers are more than instruments of poverty reduction; they are also techniques that effect a new way of governing individual conduct. My position in this article is influenced by the Foucaultian governmentality perspective which views power as productive.

The Foucaultian governmentality perspective is concerned with understanding the ways in which mundane techniques, in this case, cash transfers, effect a change in social relations and introduce new forms of governing. According to Wendy Larner, what is particularly useful about the governmentality approach is that it draws out the distinction between government and governance. While neo-liberalism has resulted in the shrinkage of government, governance itself has not been reduced (2000, p. 5). Governmentality theorists Peter Miller and Nikolas Rose state that "centers of government are multiple; it is not a question of the power of the centralized state, but of how, in relation to what mentalities and devices, by means of what intrigues, alliances and flows–is this locale or that able to act *as* a center" [their emphasis] (1992, p. 185). In this respect, governmentality is a useful approach because it avoids a top-down analysis of power and allows for a more complicated examination of governing and modes of ruling. The focus is not social control; rather, governmentality is a mode of analysis used to understand the "forms of power that subject us, the system of rule that administers us, the types of authority that master us" (Rose, 1993, p. 286). This approach examines the multiple and competing practices involved in power relations in each localized setting and power relations as affected by multiple sites of governing and regulation.

Based on market models and increased individual responsibility, neo-liberal rationality is linked to new forms of governing and managing future populations through the prudent choices of individuals. The role of government here does not disappear; rather, governing disperses outside of government state institutions, and many institutions become involved in regulating or policing the activities of individuals. Through the neo-liberal strategies of rule, located in diverse institutions, including health and welfare agencies, schools and workplaces, and communities, these individuals see themselves as responsible for managing their own well-being (Larner, 2000, p. 13). This has come to be known as a government through freedom. Progresa is examined here to see how the program intends to effect a new rationality of governing emphasizing individual prevention strategies, individual responsibility and rational choices. Under this rationale of governing, if individuals improve their lot in life, it is due to their own responsible choices; if they fail, then it is due to their lack of good choices.

METHODOLOGY

I spent seven months over a two-year period, from 1998 to 1999, in Mexico, mainly in Mexico City and Campeche, conducting fieldwork on Progresa. Mexico City was chosen because it is the center of social policy design and implementation. Campeche was chosen because it was the site of the pilot project for Progresa. Data were collected through semi-structured interviews with key policy officials working in the area of anti-poverty policies. Interviews were conducted with government officials [including top level policy bureaucrats, middle management officials and front-line implementers]. Mexican academics were also interviewed. All interviews were tape-recorded. The interviews secured data on the nature of the programs, and the ideology and vision underlying them. Information was also obtained about the programs' implementation and operationalization.

Official Mexican government documents were obtained by visiting offices and agencies; a smaller number of key statements by international agencies were obtained from the Internet and in libraries. Also consulted were World Bank World Development Reports, World Bank and Inter-American Development Bank documents on social co-investment funds, and Annual Reports. Evaluation reports from the International Food and Policy Research Institute as well as from progressive and feminist non-government organizations were also consulted. Mexican newspapers and magazines were also used, in particular, the Mexican daily, *La Jornada*.

In terms of analysis, the interviews and policy documents were reviewed to examine how the problem of poverty was framed. They were also used to explore the development of particular conceptualizations of the poor. Specific attention was paid to normative gender assumptions in the shaping of these policies.

MEXICO'S PROGRAM FOR EDUCATION, HEALTH AND NUTRITION (PROGRESA)

Progresa marked the first time that women were the privileged actors in a national anti-poverty program. It also marked the first time that money transfers had been given in-lieu of food subsidies, which gave poor women purchasing power and choice in their food selection. Progresa consisted of the following three elements:

- Monthly cash allowances or cash transfers consisting of 115 pesos were given to women to contribute to the improvement of their families' food consumption [$10 US dollars approximately].
- Monthly cash allowances were given to families as scholarships for each child under 18 enrolled in the third grade of primary school up to the third grade of secondary school. The scholarships increased for higher grades and were slightly higher for girls than boys. For a child in the 9th year of school [or third year in secondary school] grants were equal to 46% of the average earnings of an agricultural worker. An upper limit per family cap was placed on scholarship subsidies. The amount of money received by a family could vary between 115 to 525 pesos a month [between $10 to $50 US dollars per month].
- Monthly medical visits were mandatory for women and children. Women had also to attend a total of 24 health workshops on hygiene and family planning over a two-year period.

Progresa reflects the shift in political rationalities from the welfare state [interventionist and development state with protectionist economic policies] to that of the neo-liberal state [learner, cost-efficient, market-driven state which promotes competition and privatization]. Zedillo's term witnessed the re-orientation of universal subsidies and the reduction and closure of many para-state welfare institutions. For example, the universal subsidies of tortillas ended in January 1999, and the National Basic Products Company (CONASUPO) was completely closed in early 1999. The budget of the office of social development (SEDESOL) was also drastically reduced. In addition, new eligibility requirements were added to social assistance program regulations, thereby reducing the number of eligible recipients.

The Progresa program was framed in terms of individual rather than collective rights. This marked a significant departure from the official discourse which, up until then, had framed social programs in collective terms of "social solidarity" with those excluded from the spoils of the 1917 Revolution. Since the 1970s, the signature presidential anti-poverty programs including PIDER (1970-1976), COPLAMAR (1976-1982), and PRONASOL (1988-1994) incorporated a component of community participation. In particular, PRONASOL was structured on a demand-driven model of development, making it distinct from previous poverty reduction programs. That is, the poor, organized within *Comités de Solidaridad* (Committees for local Solidarity), had to present a proposal in order for production or infrastructure projects to be eligible for funding. The Progresa policy rationale centered on investment in the individual, thus the program ushered in a new conceptualization of social justice, which was understood in individual terms.

Furthermore, Progresa represented the first time that a program distinguished between the "extremely poor" and the "moderately poor." To qualify for assistance, households needed to be of low incomes, supporting many children, and lacking basic household equipment and services, such as water (Progresa, 1998, p. 17). In remote poor communities in rural Mexico, not all would be eligible to receive the benefits. This divided communities between those who received subsidies and those ineligible for cash transfers.

In sum, the actual cash transfers were small; the target population was restricted to the poorest segment among the poor; and the funds were given on the condition that the recipient agreed to participate in health and schooling programs also intended to reduce poverty. In other words, the cash transfers were less important in re-distributing resources and opportunity than they were in socializing the poor, particularly poor women, to understand themselves in a new way and to regulate their own behavior accordingly. By May 2000, the program covered 2.6 million households that included 14 million persons in 72,345 localities in all 31 states. Nevertheless, half of the extremely poor remained excluded from the program (Boltvinik, September 29, 1999). In 1999 the budget of the program was around $777 million, equivalent to just under 20% of the federal poverty alleviation budget or 0.2% of the GPD (Skoufias, Davis, & de la Vega, 2001, p. 1769).

INTELLECTUAL ORIGINS OF THE PROGRESA PROGRAM

The link between human capital development and poverty reduction has also been made by Amartya Sen, 1998 Noble Laureate. Sen's writings have greatly influenced the World Bank, the Inter-American Development Bank and Mexican anti-poverty policy, especially, the Progresa program. A central tenet of Progresa is the building of the basic capacities of the poor. According to Sen, poverty is the result of the deprivation of certain basic capacities or freedoms. He underscores the notion of human capital or basic capacities such as being well fed, healthy, educated, and sheltered. He also notes that a country's high GNP does not necessarily translate into longer and more fulfilled lives for its poor.

In conceptualizing poverty as capability deprivation, Sen demonstrates that poverty is more complicated that just measuring poverty income levels. For example, African-Americans have an absolute income higher than the population of the Indian state of Kerala. But in Kerala, citizens are better off in terms of their ability to function than African-Americans living in Harlem, New York City (Sen, 1999, p. 90-98). For Sen, investment in human capital allows people the freedom to live the lives they wish to lead and increases their abilities to participate in economic activities.

Sen's vision of human capital development involves a "partial return to an approach to economic development championed in Adam Smith's *Wealth of Nations* (1776) . . ." (1997, p. 541). Sen draws on Smith's conception of human capacities and argues that the "development of human capability and the role of experience and the division of labor were quite central to Smith's analysis of the 'wealth of nations'" (1997, p. 541). Sen, like Smith, champions the importance of the market. However, he also envisions a place where the market must be complemented with local cultures and social safety nets. For Sen, building human capital is closely linked with human freedom which is good in and of itself but "it is also a principal determinant of individual initiative and social effectiveness . . . [G]reater freedom enhances the ability of people to help themselves and also to influence the world, and these matters are central to the process of development" (1999, p. 18).

Since the 1990s, investing in human development has been part of the vocabulary of the World Bank. The World Bank's *World Development Report, 1990: Poverty* proposed [among other measures] labor-intensive growth and investment in the human capital development of the poor. This strategy of market-oriented growth for economic development and poverty alleviation continues to be a dominant concern and was repeated in a subsequent World Bank Report, the *World Development Report: Attacking Poverty 2000/1*. Similarly, the Inter-American Development Bank has directed attention to human capital development in its poverty alleviation policies. During a lecture at York University, in Ontario, the President of the IADB, Enrique Iglesias, stated that the IADB would place priority on the development of human capital in Latin America. Iglesias indicated that:

The state plays a compensatory role with respect to education and health programs in order to give power to and to empower the poor. The state needs to make people capable. The market's role is to establish discipline and it can make money, but it cannot distribute money. Therefore we need market friendly interventions to help society and markets to fulfill certain objectives, we need *intelligent government interventions, not like the old ones, but new types of state interventions.* [my emphasis] (April 3, 2000)

While Progresa is unique to Mexico, it exemplifies and is part of the new "intelligent government intervention" that is said to be investing in the human capital development of the poor. These neo-liberal social programs that are being implemented throughout Latin America, creating a more educated and healthier population of poor, do little to challenge an economic system in which the majority of the world's poor continue to be socially excluded and marginalized. The emphasis on building the basic capacities of the poor obscures the real problem of structural economic power inequalities that produce conditions of extreme wealth and poverty, poor nutrition, inadequate education, and a lack of health care for the poor.

PROGRESA: A NEO-LIBERAL SOCIAL PROGRAM

Above all, then, Progresa was part of the compensatory neo-liberal anti-poverty program, which was associated with post-developmentalist and post-paternalistic state practices. The neo-liberal model of social development is premised on the assumption that overall general well-being will be achieved by decreasing the role of the state and increasing the role of privatization as a replacement for state services and responsibilities. Different terminology accompanied the shift from social development to the neo-liberal model. In Mexico, beginning with President Miguel de la Madrid (1982-1988) but invoked more often by President Carlos Salinas (1988-1994) and Ernesto Zedillo (1994-2000), the term eradicating paternalistic practices had been used extensively in political discourse. Eradicating paternalistic practices can be seen as a flexible concept that takes on different meanings. The term was used to convey the notion that political corruption in social and political practices would be rooted out and replaced by transparent and clean governance. At the same time, the notion of eliminating paternalistic state practices was linked with the dismantling of "inefficient" universal subsidies that were associated with the bureaucratic-centralized state. The old model of state provision of subsidies was said to have created a culture of dependency.

Unlike the paternalistic subsidy programs of the developmentalist state that were thought to foster "state-dependency," Progresa, an "intelligent compensatory program," sought to empower the poor through investing in their human capital. In fact, one of the stated objectives of poverty alleviation programs in Mexico was the avoidance of dependency. Cash transfers to the families were based on amounts that would contribute to increasing household food income, but were not sufficient to meet other needs. This was designed to avoid creating a disincentive for poor families to engage in productive work (Progresa, 1998, p. 51). More specifically, in Mexico post-paternalistic state practices of prevention, freedom of choice and responsibilization for the right choices were all tied together. The Progresa program was situated in liberal discourses of the rational free adult subject who is the best, indeed the only, judge of what is in his/her interest. Progresa allowed its beneficiaries the opportunity to exercise their freedom and choice. However, their choice was regulated. Governing neo-liberal societies was about regulating populations and in this case, regulating the poor to govern themselves and thus make the choices the state wished to encourage.

The following sections explore the extent to which the program of Progresa operates according to its stated goals, namely the avoidance of dependency, resulting in the creation of active, rational and responsible citizens, able to manage their risk of greater vulnerability and poverty.

CASH TRANSFERS

This section draws attention to how cash transfers sought to create a rational actor through the presumption that recipients were afforded greater freedom to make choices, albeit limited choices. In an interview with the then deputy Minister of Finance, Santiago Levy,[5] he stated that "changing the method of purchasing power from direct food subsidies to cash transfers provided poor women with choice in their food purchases" (personal communication, February 22, 1999). Cash transfers as opposed to subsidies on foods such as tortillas and milk enabled recipients to decide for themselves how to spend their money. In other words, they could decide to purchase the food items they wanted, rather than receiving only a selected number of subsidized food staples. In this context, poor women now had a degree of autonomy.

The high incidence of drunken husbands acting irresponsibly in the past was used as a rationale to justify money transfers to women instead of men. For example, in a community Asamblea [town-hall meeting] the [male] SEDESOL representative told a gathering that "we men are irresponsible, we drink away our money. That is why women are given the cash transfers" (field notes, February 18, 1998). In official government discourse women were being constructed as more responsible than men. Therefore, they deserved the right to obtain and manage the cash transfers. At the same time, women were made responsible and accountable for their families' needs.

Monthly cash transfers of 115 pesos were provided to the mother of the eligible family specifically for the purchase of food to enhance the nutritional level of children. Poor women were required to personally collect their checks at the nearest assigned office. The bureaucratic procedures involved in collecting the money usually took an entire day. Many women had to bring their young children with them, which added to the travel and food costs. While the monies were granted for a two-month period, there was no pre-established date for the distribution of the funds. The community promoter informed the women of the dates. [The role of the community promoter will be discussed in the next section].

Cash transfers were intended to empower women. In an interview, the then National Coordinator of Progresa, Gómez de León, indicated that cash transfers "were provided to equalize the power imbalances within the family between women and men to recognize the important role that women played in their families" (personal communication, January 22, 1999). Undoubtedly there were some positive aspects to the giving of money transfers directly to women and not men. Giving money to women signaled a new way for poor women to begin seeing themselves. According to Nahmad, Carrasco and Sarmiento:

> In some cases, the money transfers have effected a change in their self-esteem and these women no longer see themselves as housewives that are limited to the confines of their houses, to wait on their families, now they are seen as the "women of Progresa" in their community and they are together because the program allows them to get organized. (1999, p. 23)

In these communities, 99% of the women indicated that they administered the monies and decided where the money was spent; only 1% of the women said they handed their monies over to their husbands

(Nahmad, Carrasco, & Sarmiento, 1999, p. 23). As the evaluation report demonstrates, it is largely in the domestic sphere where the women's decision-making authority has increased, thus reinforcing the gendered responsibilities of women within the traditional division of labor.

Cash transfers were a strategy for creating a rational actor capable of making individual and responsible choices for his/her life. In an interview, Santiago Levy, stated, "if you want the poor to behave like adults then you must treat them like adults" (personal communication, February 22, 1999). One of the objectives of the program, then, was "to induce the responsibility and the active participation of parents and all the members of the family in the pursuit of the greatest benefit of education, health and nutrition for children and young people" (Progresa, 1998, p. 39). Although the amount of the financial cash transfer allotment was small, the nexus between cash and choice was an important aspect in the production of a neo-liberal political rationality concerned with the shift from client [read: "without choices"] to consumer [read: "with choices"]. However, freedom and choice was limited to a predetermined selection of goods and services. Therefore, beneficiaries were not completely free to do whatever they wished with their cash transfers, but had to use the money in a "responsible" manner. If they did not, their subsidy could be taken away. According to a high-ranking Progresa official, 50,000 families were annually removed from the program for not meeting the program's requirements (Ballinas, Nov. 14, 2000). Thus, the threat of removal was real.

In keeping with the insights of Foucault, this understanding of freedom is situated within a productive use of the form of power (1978). Power exercised through "freedom of choice" moves away from the coercive notion of state power, and is replaced by "responsible" and "prudent" choices made by program beneficiaries. In fact, the program was based on the commitment of women beneficiaries to become co-responsible actors with the government in the actualization of the objectives of school attendance on the part of children, as well as regular family visits to the health clinic. The Progresa program represented government through freedom, which in turn represented a shift from governing through the direct administration of state institutions to that of governing through the "active" and responsible choices of individuals and their families.

PROGRESA AND THE COMMUNITY PROMOTER

The role of the community promoter was to ensure that program beneficiaries made the sanctioned choices. Communities that qualified to receive the Progresa program were required to elect a *promotora comunitaria* [community promoter], usually a woman who was fluent in Spanish,[6] to act as the liaison between the office of Progresa and the community. The *promotora* was responsible for orienting the families and informing women of important dates and events, such as picking up their checks, health visits, and performing the tasks [*faenas*] that needed to be done in the communities, among others. Indeed, the Progresa *promotora* made possible "governing at a distance" (Rose, 1999, p. 49). Rose and Miller use this term to explain that liberal rule is tied to the activities of independent authorities and experts, such as doctors, managers, and social workers (Rose, 1999, p. 49 fn 78). The term is useful here to explain that the Mexican government did not have to participate directly in these processes as the *promotoras* ensured that these women and their children were properly governed.

The *promotora* played the dual roles of leading and policing. The *promotora* informed the women of the program particulars and sometimes assumed the position of the health promoter. As health promoter, the *promotora* worked closely with officials at the health clinic and, in the absence of a clinic, worked with the mobile health unit [PAC brigade], which visited the community on a monthly basis. The health *promotora* also informed the community about future medical visits and was responsible for other related health duties. The *promotora* and the health *promotora* also informed the Program office of any problems and fraudulent activities committed by the women. The Mexican government therefore did not participate directly in these processes even though it had established the overall regulatory resources. The *promotora comunitaria*, the medical teams, and the teachers working within this framework, ensured that the poor women and their children complied with the dictates of the program.

It was the *promotora* who demanded the active participation of the beneficiaries of the program. The *promotoras comunitarias* motivated the beneficiaries to participate in health and educational programs and a range of other activities including cleaning the schools, the medical centers and neighborhoods. Participation in such activities was promoted as community development. Community participation was not a direct formal requirement, but became an informal request. Nonetheless, these community tasks became an important part of the program. Many women complained that the combination of their regular duties and these responsibilities left them with little time to take care of their own needs. This grievance was reported in a Progresa evaluation report based on 12 communities in 6 states. According to the Report:

The obligation of participating in meetings, talks, and occasional duties leaves little time to efficiently tend to their productive activities. Some have indicated that they have to attend the clinics three times a week and that only leaves them with four days, including Saturdays to work on their land. In addition, if the person rents parcels of land for the cultivation of their corn, the result is that all the duties required to pay their rent leaves them with no time to prepare the food that has been cultivated for their own self-consumption. This results in a vicious cycle in which people have become poorer. (Nahmad, Carrasco, & Sarmiento, 1999, p. 30)

It is not surprising then, that the *promotora comunitaria* in her role as instigator and regulator of these tasks was not always liked in her community.

PREVENTATIVE HEALTH CARE MANAGEMENT

The Progresa program brought a new focus on health and shifted the concern from illness-care to preventative care. Illness-care was concerned only with curing the malnourished and ill patient. The focus of preventative care was reducing the risk to the healthy person of becoming ill through proper nutrition and regular medical examinations. It was a pro-active approach to health. As stated in the Progresa document, "the focus is to train women in better nutrition and to instill in them responsible habits of preventative health care" (Progresa, 1998, p. 47). The intended outcome was an active and rational woman who understood the importance of prevention and self-care.

Progresa required that poor women and their children regularly attended health clinics. In addition, women were expected to attend a total of 24 health workshops on hygiene and family planning over a two-year period. In these workshops, women were taught the importance of preventative care and cleanliness, including food preparation and housework. Medical professionals and social workers recorded the attendance of women in the various activities [S1 health forms were used to incorporate families into the program]. Failure to participate in any activity resulted in the loss of benefits. A specially designed formula [or *papilla*] was available for pregnant women, nursing mothers and malnourished children up until the age of 5.

Rural communities did not have a uniform health infrastructure. The health component of the Progresa program was made available through three existing programs. Some communities had an established IMSS-Solidaridad health clinic [begun as the IMSS-COPLAMAR program] which, in some cases, had been operating for over twenty years. IMSS-Solidaridad clinics were administered by staff, including a nurse, a health auxiliary [or *promotora comunitaria*] and another volunteer. The local community assisted with the overall maintenance of the clinic. The doctors attended to emergencies and more serious illnesses in hospitals in the larger rural communities. Other communities had clinics which were affiliated with the Ministry of Health (SSA). A relatively recent medical option for some in rural communities was attaining health services from the *Programa de Ampliación de Cobertura* (PAC) [program of extended coverage].

The ambition of state intervention was the creation of the responsible subject who engaged in practices of preventative health-care. The interview with the director of the PAC program in Campeche, Dr. Martinez, echoed many of the intentions of the federal government. Dr. Martinez glowingly spoke about PAC and Progresa as programs that finally offered a health safety net for the poor. In an interview, Dr. Martinez stated that "the objective of PAC and Progresa was to educate the population so that they could see the benefits of participating in their own self-care" (personal communication, February 21, 1998). This means that the poor were taught to make the right choices. The training or *capacitación* took place in the health workshops. Dr. Martinez stated that "we need to train people to change their behavior," adding that "we don't want girls taken out of schools so that they stay home to make tortillas, nor do we want to see girls getting married young and once married we hope that they choose family planning methods" (personal communication, February 21, 1998). Others commented on how Progresa was creating a culture of health-prevention. In the Mexican daily, *La Jornada*, another medic, Dr. Urbina indicated, "Progresa is effecting a fundamental change in the attitudes of people. Before, doctors attended the sick; now they monitor healthy families" (Editorial, Nov. 16, 1998).

While there was much discussion about preventative care, there was little medical infrastructure–health-clinics, staff, and supplies–to support it. In fact, Martha Castañeda, who evaluated the PAC program in two indigenous municipalities in Oaxaca, concluded that the program did not have the sufficient fiscal resources to offer the most basic services for health care.[7] The report indicated that both the training program and the supplies of the health promoters were inadequate. Her findings suggested that there were not enough health auxiliaries [or promoters] to meet their communities' demands. Consequently, most promoters were overworked. The health workshops, which were supposed to be geared toward the educational health training of the family, were actually directed at training women in health care strategies. Health training workshops were responsibilizing poor women to assume greater involvement in the care of their families. While some knowledge about health was gained through these workshops, the result was an increased gendering of health care responsibilities.

Many women felt patronized in the health workshops. As one women stated: "we have to clean the clinic when its our turn and in the talks they tell us that we shouldn't be pigs, that we need to bathe daily and to cut our finger nails" (Nahmad, Carrasco, & Sarmiento, 1999, p. 19). In Castañeda's interviews, a health promoter indicated that "people are tired of talks on boiling the water and on getting rid of old and non useful things . . . yet there are no medicines" [Auxiliar de Salud, in Castañeda, 1999, p. 30]. Moreover, in the same evaluation study, it was reported that the PAC brigades did not have sufficient supplies to carry out proper medical health examinations. For example, the report stated that tests for cervical cancer were no longer being performed, as no lab technician was available to interpret the findings (Castañeda, 1999, p. 35).

Discourses about health prevention masked the reform of the state. The health workshops facilitated the politics of transferring state social responsibilities to poor women and their families. These shifts in state responsibility engendered the feminization of health care. In other words, poor women with little training and resources were made to provide their communities with health services. In her observations, Castañeda states:

> The commitment to increase the level of health of the population as the task of the state is transferred to citizens: the health of poor citizens is the responsibility of women that have been trained. The attention to sickness for those with better levels of well-being depends on their own economic resources. (Castañeda, 1999, p. 7)

Thus, for basic care, local poor women would cater to the needs of the ill. For advanced care, the state would provide some services, but was also encouraging the privatization of health-care in the rural areas.

EDUCATION AND SCHOLARSHIPS

Educating the children of the poor was seen as a long-term strategy intended to break the "vicious cycle of poverty." In selected Progresa families, the mothers of children between the ages of 8 to 17 years [who were between the third year of primary and the third year of secondary school] completed a form [E1, *Constancia de Inscripción*] to receive a scholarship. This form, which was also signed by the teacher, was submitted to the Progresa office by the *promotora comunitaria* or the municipal office. Teachers at the rural schools were required to keep detailed attendance sheets that were submitted on a monthly basis to the Progresa office. A total of 29 absent days over an academic year would result in the suspension of the scholarship. Absences for illness would be recognized only if a medical certificate was provided.

Progresa scholarships were designed to accomplish a number of objectives, including the lowering of the extremely high, school attrition rates.[8] Another objective was the equalization of gender differences. In an interview, Gómez de León, stated "scholarships must accomplish the objectives of social justice by equalizing the opportunities between men and women" (personal communication, January 22, 1999). As part of the Progresa program, scholarships were given as incentives for parents to send their children to school and to not pull them out of school to supplement the household income. The risk of pulling children out of school was mitigated by financial incentives. Therefore, parents were to understand that paying children to go to school was equivalent to having them work in the fields. It was hoped that this would prevent further illiteracy. These transfers made poor families responsible through investing in their human capacities [in education] and thereby avoiding short-term risk solutions, such as pulling children out of school. Moreover, teachers used their class rosters to ensure that children and their mothers abided by the rules of their scholarships.

Education was linked to the actualization of the objectives of social justice, which included building the human capital of children so they could take advantage of future opportunities. In an interview, Levy indicated that the poor had to be incorporated into the labor force and that education was the necessary vehicle for preparing the poor to take advantage of emergent economic opportunities. Levy postulated that "Mexico needs for the poor to be integrated into productive life and cannot afford to maintain 25% of its population that does not contribute to national welfare or national output" (personal communication, March 3, 1999).

The Mexican government was hoping for a convergence of a better skilled and better-educated labor force and a prosperous, economic market, able to employ future generations of workers. While these were laudable objectives, much of this reasoning depended on a healthy economic environment which until now had been unable to incorporate the poor into productive life. However, the problem was that since 1982 Mexico had been in a deep economic recession. Therefore, any discussion about incorporating the excluded poor into the economic growth of the country was premature. More problematic, however, was the assumption that the completion of primary and secondary education would lead to improved income opportunities. To begin with, a change in the educational profile of millions of people would not likely impact on the market, and was not likely to create better-paying jobs for millions of poor people. More pointedly, according to World Bank findings in Mexico, there were only sustainable increases in income for those who completed preparatory and university levels of education. Completion of primary and secondary levels of education did not result in increased earning power (Boltvinik, May 26, 2000).

GOVERNING THROUGH THE INDIVIDUAL AND THE DISRUPTION OF COMMUNITY

The Progresa program had not only interrupted individual lives, it had disrupted community life as well by dividing families. As a Progresa functionary in Campeche noted, "inside the communities there exists a division between those that have the support and those–the other poor–who do not qualify" (personal communication, February 15, 1999). María de Jesús, a Progresa beneficiary from San Luis Potosí, angrily describes Progresa as a program that "serves to divide us" (Cano & Cervantes, 1998). She asks:

> Why is the money not equal? Why don't we all receive this money? Why? We don't know, if we are all equally screwed. And why is the money conditioned on doing tasks? (Ibid.)

In addition to creating conflict among families, Progresa also interrupted traditional community practices. In the past, all decisions, including the management of a government program, were made during meetings in the community *Asamblea*. During the *Asamblea*, the community members would decide how the program would operate in their community. This was not a romantic process of community life. As Fernando Guadarrama Olivera points out, there have always been conflicts and tensions in the community. However, the decisions arrived at in the *Asamblea* were respected. Guadarrama Olivera profiled Progresa recipients in the community of *San Francisco Xitlama*, in the municipality of *Zoquitlán*, in the *Sierra Negra de Puebla* (December, 1998). His findings suggest that Progresa, as a program, entered the community as a complete package in which bureaucrats have made the central decisions.

Friction and social tension has been the result of providing some poor families and not others with cash transfers, scholarships and health-care services. Michelle Adato from the International Food Policy Research Institute (IFPRI) evaluated the program and her finding indicated that the Progresa program caused many social problems within communities. In fact, the Progresa program effected the creation of social tensions, defined in Adato's report as resentment, envy or gossip, in many communities that have come to be known as Progresa communities (2000, p. 32). Also, according to her findings, the social tension in the community was referred to as " 'the community is not well', and there is a desire for everyone to be part of the program so that they 'will all be fine'" (Adato, 2000, p. vii). In her conclusion, Adato stated that community members preferred programs that provided "equally for all members," rather than programs that were concerned with "equity." Adato points out "the social costs of targeting at the household level may be high in these communities where the distinctions made by the program between poor and extreme, or needing assistance and not needing assistance, are not apparent in the view of the people who live there, who see themselves as 'all poor' and 'all in need'" (2000, p. 32). This study, while not surprising, confirms that social tension will result when resources are not given equally to all poor families that live in very similar conditions of poverty, many of whom lived in marginalized and isolated communities.

Based on the various evaluations, it appears that the Progresa program has caused much discord within indigenous communities. There seems to be a convergence between the investment in the development of human capital of the poor, in the production of an active, responsible individual that can manage his/her own risk of greater poverty and vulnerability, and in the freeing of the individual from affective or communal ties. The enabled and rational [read: "modern"] individual is no longer conditioned by customs and traditions but is able to associate with other networks, associations and organizations. Re-casting the subjectivity of the poor also entails changing his/her traditional mentalities, organizations, and ways of life. The concern here is to produce an "individual who has no other 'public' ties than contractual ones he chooses for himself" (Williams & Young, 1994, p. 98). Thus, the modern individual is one who actively makes rational and responsible choices, which are independent of kinship structures, communal ties and traditions.

DID PROGRESA REDUCE POVERTY?

Program evaluations were carried out by the Mexican government in collaboration with the International Food and Policy Research Institute in Washington. Beginning in 1998, twenty-four months were spent evaluating the program. The states of Guerrero, Hidalgo, Michoacán, Puebla, Querétaro, San Luis Potosí, and Veracruz were included in the evaluation study. The following is an outline of some of the general findings. Educational enrollment had increased and the presence of girls at the secondary school level had also increased (Schultz cited in Skoufias & McClafferty, 2000, p. 3). The results implied that children would have, on average, about 0.7 years of extra schooling and this was said to increase future earnings by 8% (Skoufias & McClafferty, 2000, p. 3). An overall improvement in health was cited and the report indicated that children had a 12% lower incidence of illness. Adults reported a 19% decrease in sick or disability days (Gertler cited in Skoufias & McClafferty, 2000, p. 3). The nutritional level of children seemed to improve and this was said to have an effect on reducing the probability of stunting growth for children aged 12 to 36 months (Behrman & Hoddinott cited in Skoufias & McClafferty, 2000, p. 3). Also reported was an increase in food consumption, in terms of both calorie intake and a diversified diet (Skoufias & McClafferty, 2000, p. 3). With regard to the empowerment of women, the findings indicate, "women report a greater level of empowerment, defined as increased self confidence and control over their movements and household resources" (Skoufias & McClafferty, 2000, p. 3).

The general tone of the IFPRI evaluation report was one of optimism, suggesting that many of the program impacts "are likely to manifest themselves in the future" (Skoufias & McClafferty, 2000, p. 3). This begs the question, how significant was the nutritional, educational and empowerment impact of the Progresa evaluation. With a program whose results can only be assessed in the future, it is difficult to measure impact only after a few years of implementation. A more accurate evaluation needs to be based on a longitudinal study, which examines a Progresa community for a period of 5 years and evaluates the results in terms of changes in health and nutritional levels in that area during the period. Only then can it be determined whether the program was successful in the reduction of poverty.

CONCLUSION

Progresa is an example of trends in neo-liberal anti-poverty programs concerned with human capital development and poverty alleviation. Progresa emphasizes attention to equalizing gender imbalances and positions women and children as key beneficiaries. Progresa was designed as a future-oriented program intended to break the "vicious cycle of poverty" through interventionist measures of cash transfers, scholarships, and preventative health care. Progresa cash transfers hoped to effect a new subjectivity of poor women from the passive recipient of indirect subsidies to the empowered market subject who is now given freedom through cash transfers to make choices about her food purchases. Making the wrong choice, such as spending money on alcohol or paying old debts would entail consequences. Moreover, poor women's in-kind contributions and compulsory volunteerism was also directly tied to receiving benefits. That is, women had to engage in the required community activities such as cleaning the medical clinics and the schools.

Cash transfers have opened up spaces for new ways of governing the conduct of the poor and also for the poor to govern their conduct. If women do not follow the rules, they risk losing cash transfers for food and scholarships for their children. Progresa represented government through "freedom." Poor women were governed through their "responsible choices," within a system that defined what was responsible and virtually forced them to comply. While the state theoretically relinquished its role as the expert manager in needs-management and viewed the poor as adults with choices, the program requirements continued to regulate the lives of the poor through medical attendance sheets and class rosters. Thus, the Mexican state continues to govern the poor through the choices they make. Human capital, choice and freedom, which were productive forms of power, operated simultaneously with coercive, punitive and disciplinary forms of power that sought to responsibilize poor women in the management of their own poverty.

Interestingly, not all poor families were upset at their exclusion from the Progresa program. A poor woman from Campeche spoke on behalf of many when she mentioned the relief she felt at being excluded from the program. She stated:

> Thank God! We are not part of the Progresa program.
> We are free from the pressure to attend meetings and the obligatory workshops. And the money is very little. (Red Nacional de Promotoras y Asesoras Rurales, April 2000, p. 6)

Progresa, a program that sought to build the human capabilities of poor women and their children, facilitated the replacement of the welfare state apparatus with limited and regulated choices. The program that was touted as the great gender equalizer, in fact facilitated the greater entrenchment of uncontested notions of gendered activities with increased regulation and limited choices. The program exemplifies trends in poverty alleviation that focus heavily on investing in people, particularly women and children, without questioning the economic policies of market oriented growth and trade agreements that perpetuate the problem of poverty and inequality. In a neo-liberal context, the concept of human capital masks the reform of the state, disrupts social relations, as was seen in the indigenous communities, and places greater emphasis on poor individuals to manage their own poverty.

NOTES

1. Some examples are the Honduras Family Assistance Program (1995) and Argentina's Support for Youth Productivity and Employability (1997), which provide cash incentives to keep children in schools (Lustig & Deutsch, 1998, 21). The Brazilian *Bolsa Escola* program provides scholarships to children that live in communities with high levels of child labor. Nicaragua's *Red de Protección Social* has a similar design as Progresa and Colombia's *Apoyo Familiar* program offers a number of interventions. The Bangladesh Food-for-Education program provides 100 kilograms of rice as incentives for children to attend school.

2. Under Vicente Fox's government (2000-2006) the Progresa program was replaced by a similar program called *Oportunidades* (Opportunities). Under the new program coverage was extended to households in poor and marginalized urban areas.

3. The author is responsible for the translation of all Spanish sources used in this article, including interviews, government and non-government documents, academic literature, and newspaper articles.

4. In Canadian/American terms, it would be between grades 3 and 9.

5. Santiago Levy's influential document, Poverty Alleviation in Mexico: a Working Paper for the World Bank (1991), set the context for the direction of Mexican anti-poverty policy and in particular the Progresa program.

6. In remote rural areas in Mexico many indigenous peoples speak their native dialect. They do not speak Spanish.

7. The study forms part of a larger investigation called "Promoviendo la participación de la mujer en los proyectos sociales contra la pobreza financiados por el

Banco Mundial" carried out between September 1996 to May 1998 in Oaxaca for Trasparencia S.C under the general coordination of Suman Battacharjea.

8. According to poverty expert Julieta Campos, there was a 40% school dropout rate in urban areas and a rate of 80% in rural areas. Campos argues that a "good part of the social budget" benefits sections of the population that were living in extreme poverty and the budget for education was far from arriving at the recommendations set by UNESCO that determined that 8% of the GNP should have been dedicated to education. In Mexico between the years 1995 and 1997 the percentage of the budget for education did not surpass 5% (Herrera Beltarán, November 11, 1998).

REFERENCES

Adato, M. (2000). *The Impact of Progresa on Community Social Relationships*. Retrieved on August 2001 from http://www.ifpri.org/themes/progresa/household.html

Alvarez, S. E. (1996). Concluding Reflections 'Redrawing' the Parameters of Gender Struggle. In J. Friedmann et al (Ed.), *Emergences: Women's Struggles for livelihood in Latin America* (pp. 137-151). Los Angeles: UCLA Latin American Center Publications, University of California.

Alvarez, S. E. (1998, March). *Advocating Feminism: The Latin American Feminist NGO 'Boom,'* Retrieved March 23, 2000, from http://www.mtholyoke.edu/acad/latam/schomburgmoreno/alvarez.html

Ballinas, V. (2000, November 14). Los programas contra la pobreza, en un mar de miseria creciente. *La Jornada*. Retrieved same day from http://www.jornada.unam.mx/2000/nov00/001114/040n1soc.html

Barrig, M. (1996). Women, Collective Kitchens, and the Crisis of the State in Peru. In J. Friedmann et al. (Ed.), *Emergences: Women's Struggles for livelihood in Latin America* (pp. 59-77). Los Angeles: UCLA Latin American Center Publications, University of California.

Barrig, M. (1998). Female Leadership, Violence, and Citizenship in Peru. In J. Jaquette and S. L. Wolchik (Ed.), *Women and Democracy* (pp. 104-124). Baltimore: The Johns Hopkins University Press.

Bisnath, S., & Elson, D. (2000). Women's Empowerment Revisited. In *Progress of the World's Women, 2000*. United Nations Development Fund for Women. Retrieved February 2001 from http://www.unifem.undp.org/progressww/papers.html

Blondet, C. (1995). Out of the Kitchens and onto the Streets: Women's Activism in Peru. In A. Basu (Ed.), *The Challenge of Local Feminisms* (pp. 251-275). Boulder, Colorado: Westview Press, Inc.

Boltvinik, J. (1999, September 29). Los excluidos del Progresa. *La Jornada*. Retrieved same day from http://www.jornada.unam.mx/1999/sep99/990913/oja- excluidos. html

Boltvinik, J. (2000, May 26). Evaluando el Progresa. *La Jornada*. Retrieved same day from http://www.jornada.unam.mx/2000/may00/000526/boltvinik.html

Cano, A. & Cervantes, J. (1998, November 15). Viaje al "focalizado" combate a la probreze. ¿Quién progresa con el Progresa? *La Jornada*. Retrieved same day from http://www.jornada.unam.mx/1998/nov98/981115/mas-progresa51.html

Castañeda, M. A. (1999, November). *El Programa de Ampliación de Cobertura en Comunidades Indígenas de Oaxaca: participatión comunitaria y perspectiva de género.* Centro de Estudios de la Mujer y la Familia, A.C. Oaxaca, Mexico, unpublished report.

Cordera Campos, R. (2000, December 31). Pobreza en Progresa? *La Jornada.* Retrieved same day from http://www.jornada.unam.mx/2000/dic00/001231/ 012a1pol.html

Dieterlen, P. (1998). Progresa y la atención a las necesidades básicas. In Pilar Grediaga and Daniel Hernández (Ed.), *Alivio a la Probreza. Memoria del Seminario* (pp. 130-143). Mexico City: Centro de Investigaciones y Estudios Superiores en Antropología (CIESAS).

Editorial. (1998, November 16). *La Jornada* Retrieved same day from http://www. jornada.unam.mx/1998/nov98/981116/index.html

Foucault, M. (1978). *The History of Sexuality Volume I: An Introduction.* New York: Vintage Books.

Gómez de León, J. (1997). El Programa de Educación, Salud y Alimentación: Progresa. *El economista mexicano. Revista del Colegio Nacional de Economistas. Nueva época.,* Vol. 1, no. 4. pp. 271-282.

Guadarrama Olivera, F. (1998, December). *Perfil de la Comunidad de San Francisco Xitlama, Municipio de Zoquitlán, de la Sierra Negra de Puebla.* Mexico, unpublished report.

Herrera Béltran, C. (1998, November 11). Julieta Campos: "buena parte" del gasto social no va a los pobres. *La Jornada.* Retrieved same day from http://www.jornada. unam.mx/1998/nov98/981111/julieta.html

Jelin, E. (Ed.). (1990). *Women and Social Change in Latin America.* London: Zed Books Limited.

Larner, W. (2000). Neo-liberalism: Policy, Ideology, Governmentality. *Studies in Political Economy,* 63, pp. 5-25.

Levy, Santiago. (1991, May) Poverty Alleviation in Mexico. *Working Papers.* The World Bank, WPS 679.

Lind, A C. (1992). Power, Gender, and Development: Popular Women's Organizations and the Politics of Needs in Ecuador. In A. Escobar & S. E. Alvarez (Ed.), *The Making of social movements in Latin America: identity, strategy, and democracy* (pp. 134-149). Boulder: Westview Press.

Lind, A & Farmelo, M. (1996, June). Gender and Urban Social Movements: Women's Community Responses to Restructuring and Urban Poverty. *United Nations Research Institute for Social Development, Discussion Paper No. 76.* Retrieved on March 23, 2000 from http://www.unrisd.org/unrisd/website/document.nsf/ (httpPublications)/C59D935EC5987D6180256B65004FF007?OpenDocument

Lind, A. (1997). Gender, Development and Urban Social Change: Women's Community Action in Global Cities. *World Development,* vol 25. no. 8, pp. 1205-1223.

Luccisano, L. (2001). Communal Kitchens in Peru and Mexico. In K. Hunt & C. Saulnier (Ed.), *Feminism(s) on the Edge of the Millennium* (pp. 39-54). Toronto: Inanna Publications Inc.

Miller, P. & Rose, N. (1992). Political Power beyond the State: Problematics of Government. *British Journal of Sociology,* 43 no. 2. pp. 172-205.

Nahmad, S., Carrasco, T, & Sarmiento, S. (1999, January 15) *Acercmiento Ethnografico Y Cultural Sobre El Impacto Del Programa Progresa En Doce Comunidades de Seis Estados De La Republica. Ciesas Unidad Istmo.* Oaxaca, Mexico, unpublished report.

Progresa. (1998). Programa de Educación, Salud y Alimentación.

Red Nacional de Promotoras y Asesoras Rurales. (2000, April). *"Dinero Del Diablo" Ejercicio de revisión de la perspectiva de género en la Programa de Alimentación Educación y Salud (Progresa).* Mexico, unpublished report.

Rose, N. (1993). Government, Authority and Expertise in Advanced Liberalism. *Economy and Society,* 22, 3 pp. 283-299.

Rose, N. (1999). *Powers of Freedom.* Cambridge: Cambridge University Press.

Rowlands, J. (1997). *Questioning Empowerment: Working with Women in Honduras.* Oxford, England: Oxfam.

Schild, V. (1998). New Subjects of Rights? Women's Movements and the Construction of Citizenship in the 'New Democracies.' In S. E. Alvarez, E. Dagnino, & A. Escobar (Ed.), *Cultures of Politics/Politics of Culture* (pp. 93-117). Boulder, Co.: Westview Press.

Schild, V. (2000a). Neo-liberalism's New Gendered Market Citizens: The 'Civilizing' Dimension of Social Programmes in Chile. *Citizenship Studies,* vol. 4., no 3. pp. 275-305.

Schild, V. (2000b). "Gender Equity" Without Social Justice Women's Rights in the Neo-liberal Age. *NACLA Report on the Americas.* Vol. 34 (1), pp. 25-30.

Schild, V. (2001). Engendering the New Social Citizenship in Chile: NGOs and Social Provisioning under Neo-liberalism. *United Nations Research Institute for Social Development, UNRISD,* Retrieved on March 2002 from www.unrisd.org.

Sen, A. (1997). Development Thinking at the Beginning of the XXI Century. In L. Emmerij (Ed.), *Economic and Social Development in the XXI Century* (pp. 531-551). Washington, DC: Inter-American Development Bank.

Sen, A. (1999). *Development as Freedom.* New York: Alfred A. Knopf.

Skoufias, E., & McClafferty B. (2000). Is Progresa Working? Summary of the Results of an Evaluation by IFPRI. *Discussion Paper Brief 118, Food Consumption and Nutrition Division, IFPRI* Washington, D.C. Retrieved on July 2001 from http://www.ifpri.org/checknames.cfm/Skoufias_results.pdf?name=Skoufias_results. pdf&direc=d:\webs\ifpri\themes\progresa\pdf

Skoufias, E., Davis, B, & de la Vega, S (2001). Targeting the Poor in Mexico: An Evaluation of the Selection of Households into PROGRESA. *World Development,* vol 29, Issue 10, October, pp. 1769-1784.

Townsend, J., Zapata, E., Rowlands, J., Alberti, P., & Mercado, M. (1999). *Women and Power.* London: Zed Books.

Williams, D., & Young, T. (1994). Governance, the World Bank and Liberal Theory. *Political Studies.* vol. 42, no. 1 pp. 84-100.

World Bank. (1990). *World Development Report 1990: Poverty.* New York: Oxford University Press.

World Bank. (2001). *World Development Report 2000/2001 Attacking Poverty.* New York: Oxford University Press.

U.S. Navy versus Vieques, Puerto Rico: Social Justice Through Civil Disobedience

Carmen I. Aponte

SUMMARY. For over 60 years, the island of Vieques, Puerto Rico, served as a live munitions target range for the United States Navy. The Navy protected the U.S. Empire's colonial relationship with Puerto Rico. Within this context, the colonial, racial and oppressive paradigms shield most anti-military movements in Puerto Rico. The tragedy of a civilian killed in Vieques by an errant 500-pound bomb destroyed this protective shield, bringing to light the social, economical and environmental injustices and atrocities committed by the U.S. Navy. This tragedy increased the public awareness of how people's lives, beaches, environment, and livelihood had been destroyed. Social action by solidarity and civil disobedience proved powerful in the anti-military struggle for achieving justice for the people in Vieques. This paper provides an overview of the people's struggle against the U.S. Navy. The historic demilitarization of Vieques will commemorate the solidarity of people in their victory for justice and world peace. *[Article copies available for a fee from The Haworth Document Delivery Service: 1-800-HAWORTH. E-mail address: <docdelivery@haworthpress.com> Website: <http://www.HaworthPress.com> © 2004 by The Haworth Press, Inc. All rights reserved.]*

Carmen I. Aponte, PhD, is Assistant Professor, Department of Social Work, State University of New York, College at Brockport, Brockport, NY 14420 (E-mail: caponte@brockport.edu).

The author thanks Henry I. Padrón for sharing his knowledge on the history of Puerto Rico and Vieques.

[Haworth co-indexing entry note]: "U.S. Navy versus Vieques, Puerto Rico: Social Justice Through Civil Disobedience." Aponte, Carmen I. Co-published simultaneously in *Journal of Poverty* (The Haworth Press, Inc.) Vol. 8, No. 4, 2004, pp. 59-73; and: *Poverty and Inequality in the Latin American-U.S. Borderlands: Implications of U.S. Interventions* (ed: Keith M. Kilty, and Elizabeth A. Segal) The Haworth Press, Inc., 2004, pp. 59-73. Single or multiple copies of this article are available for a fee from The Haworth Document Delivery Service [1-800-HAWORTH, 9:00 a.m. - 5:00 p.m. (EST). E-mail address: docdelivery@haworthpress.com].

Digital Object Identifier: 10.1300/J134v08n04_04

KEYWORDS. U.S. Navy, Vieques, Puerto Rico, anti-military movement, civil disobedience, social, economic and environmental justice, colonialism

. . . with their people and defending their people, David has once again overcome Goliath.

–The Christian Century Foundation, 2003, p. 15

The end of the U.S. military presence in Vieques, Puerto Rico, represents a historical event for Puerto Rico, the Caribbean and Latin America. This event astonished other countries as its leaders recognized that in the midst of U.S. intervention in Iraq, the people of Puerto Rico defeated the U.S. Navy. Civil disobedience, social action and solidarity were tactics used in the struggle to demilitarize the island of Vieques. The most effective weapon was the strength behind the Puerto Rican united front. Never before has there been a cause so great and powerful that would embrace both islanders and mainland Puerto Ricans. Solidarity, collective action, and a national identity were instrumental in achieving social, economic and environmental justice for the people of Vieques (*Viequenses*).

The author intends to provide an overview of the island municipality of Vieques, Puerto Rico, and its struggle with the United States Navy. The militarization of Vieques is just one dimension of the colonial relationship between Puerto Rico and the U.S. empire. Since the 1940s, the U.S. Navy has used Vieques for military maneuvers. The raw disregard for the rights of the people and the land of Vieques exhibits the injustices committed by the U.S. for the sake of power and imperial expansion. The author wishes to alert the reader that to provide a daily account of the Vieques movement falls beyond the scope of this paper. What the author hopes to achieve is an understanding of the challenges that the Vieques anti-military movement faced in the struggle for social justice and peace in Vieques.

PRE-COLONIALISM

The history of Puerto Rico's colonial status begins with the Spanish invasion on November 19, 1493. The roots of Spanish colonialism spread onward as Spain declared sovereignty over Vieques in 1524.

Neither Puerto Rico nor Vieques were exempt from the destruction of its indigenous people and the exploitation of African slaves. The imposition of Christianity on the indigenous Taíno population justified the mistreatment and the brutality of this colonial era. Over 45,000 of the island's indigenous population were slaughtered (Padrón, 1989). A series of Royal Decrees was enacted to limit the rights of the Taíno and African people of Puerto Rico, which by virtue increased the wealth and power of the colonizer, the church and the Spanish government. Officially, slaves could not obtain freedom by marrying someone who was free, could not walk alone at night; no appeal would be granted to those Indians and slaves condemned to death; mulattos or black people could not have Indian servants, slaves nor hold public office, etc. (Padrón, 1989, pp. 40-41). By 1530, 331 Spanish Colonizers owned or had control over almost 5,000 people of color (López, 1974, p. 21; Padrón, 1989, p. 41); 30,000 slaves, by 1834 (Silén, 1971, p. 25). Thus, the colonial foundation upon which Puerto Rico would be governed during the next 400 years was set.

Puerto Ricans protested violently the harsh and repressive treatment by the Spaniards. One historical uprising but short lived was *El Grito de Lares* on September 23, 1868. At least 400 patriots and other revolutionary leaders stood up against the Spanish colonial regime and fought for their autonomy from Spain and for the abolishment of slavery. The Spanish army quickly repressed the Puerto Rican quest for independence and emancipation (Jiménez de Wagenheim, 1997). In Vieques, after officially becoming part of Puerto Rico in 1843 (McCaffrey, 2002, p. 21), the free Black English speaking workers and the African slaves also rebelled in 1864 and 1874 (Rabin, n.d.). Even after the abolishment of slavery in 1873, Spain continued to persecute the Puerto Rican autonomists.

The end of the 19th century marked a turning point in the history of Puerto Rico. Although Spain granted autonomy to Puerto Rico on February 9, 1898, by July of that same year, U.S. armed forces occupied the island during their war against Spain. In August, as a result of the Spanish-American war, Spain agreed to cede Puerto Rico to the United States (Ribes Tovar, 1973, pp. 370-378). With this war, Cuba received its independence while Puerto Rico continued its subjugated state. By the end of 1898, the U.S. expanded its empire and colonized Guam, the Philippines and Puerto Rico (Barreto, 2002; Murillo, 2001). Puerto Rico became the "hapless victim of an explosive U.S. drive to assert military and naval hegemony in the Caribbean" (McCaffrey, 2002, p. 22). As part of Puerto Rico, the U.S. empire stretched to include Vieques and its sister island Culebra. These two islands are geographically located between Puerto Rico and the U.S. Virgin Islands of St. Thomas and St. John. By the turn of the century, Culebra and Vieques were used for military maneuvers and offshore training facilities for the east coast military base, Roosevelt Roads. One type of maneuver was to target and shoot bombs from Vieques to Culebra. Eventually, the islands became laboratories for military and commercial ends.

COLONIAL STATUS

The colonial status of Puerto Rico constitutes the milieu for the historical resistance against the U.S. Navy. Deception and subjugation are some methods used for colonization (Yellow Bird, 2001). Since 1898, the American Empire colonized and disempowered Puerto Ricans in their quest for self-determination. By 1917, without being given a choice in the matter, Puerto Ricans were declared U.S. citizens (Jones Act). "Racialist constructions of Anglo-Saxon superiority were central ideological rationalizations for denying Puerto Ricans a decisive role in their own society" (Barreto, 2002, p. 13). This colonial, racial and oppressive paradigm permeated throughout the social, economic and political realms of Puerto Rico. The radical left historically resisted such ideology, struggling for Puerto Rico's self-determination and national identity against the U.S. Empire.

Another conscious or unconscious colonial tactic is the deception that any small island in the Caribbean, as Puerto Rico, cannot survive in a macroworld without the U.S. (Conway, 1998). As stated by Silén (1971), "the first lesson a schoolboy learns is that we are small, as if our smallness were not something positive for grappling with the problems of communication, electrification, irrigation, and highways" (p. 15). The military's presence in the Caribbean served to enable this state of dependency, powerlessness, constant fear, and therefore, perpetuate Puerto Rico's colonial status.

By 1943, the U.S. Navy possessed 21,000 of Vieques' 33,000 acres (Berman Santana, 2002, p. 39). The transformation from an agrarian to an industrialized society in Puerto Rico was paralleled by the growing presence of the military in Vieques. This transformation favored the U.S. economy by limiting Puerto Rico's competition in the global market, thus creating an economic crisis. The U.S. provided federal funds to relieve poverty and the unemployment rate in Puerto Rico (Dietz, 1986, Ch. 3). Such welfare programs as the Puerto Rican Emergency Relief Administration (PRERA) and the Puerto Rican Reconstruction Administration (PRRA) temporarily pacified the poor and unemployed while the growing U.S. industrial empire received military protection. However, Puerto Rico's economic ills were seen as a population growth problem (History Task Force, 1979, p.119). Three strategic programs that sought to solve such economic ills were Operation Bootstrap, Population Control, and Migration Propaganda (Nieves-Falcón, 1975, p. 11). Operation Bootstrap, the strategy used for transforming Puerto Rico's agrarian economy into an industrialized one, lured U.S. industrial enterprises through a 10 to 17 year period of tax exemption. Population Control, geared to the lower class, informed the public and provided access to birth control methods (Ramírez de Arellano & Seipp, 1983). Largely induced by U.S. Labor Contracts after World War II, migration became the 'escape valve' of the population problem. What appeared to be a migrant's quest for social and economic prospect was in fact a constant flow of cheap labor responding to the economic opportunities between the U.S. and Puerto Rico. The greatest population exodus occurred between 1940-1960 (Maldonado-Denis, 1972, p. 315).

At that time, in contrast to the population growth of the island, Vieques experienced its greatest population decline. During this post-depression era, some Viequenses anticipated that the military would create more jobs, while the eviction process devastated others, contributing further to the Puerto Rican diaspora. Many evicted Viequenses took part in Puerto Rico's 1940-1960's population exodus. Other Viequenses, attracted by the sugar cane industry, moved eastward to St. Croix. Unfortunately, St. Croix was found to be as economically depressing as Vieques (McCaffrey, 2002, p. 26). The Navy expropriated most of the remaining families to assigned plots. Each family had to sign a statement indicating that they understood the Navy's rights to repossess these lots when needed (Acevedo-Delgado, n.d.; Rabin, n.d.). McCaffrey (2002) captures Carlos Zenón, an anti-militarist activists and head of the fishermen's association, powerful narrative of the eviction process when he was a four-year old:

> I remember the day we received the notice giving us 24 hours to move because we were being expropriated. My parents were divorced and I lived with my mother, a brother and a sister. At first my mother could not believe that after living her entire life there, they could suddenly tell her to leave . . . She did not know where to go or what to do with the house. Our house was made of wood and zinc, rather small for us but comfortable. She decided not to believe what was happening and to remain. But the following day they returned and told her that they had warned her.

They told my mother that she had to leave immediately. She asked to where. She explained that she had three small children and no means of transportation. They simply gave her a form indicating that . . . a small lot of land had been set aside for her . . . and four numbers indicating the four corners of the lot. Nothing more. . . . They told her to leave because they were going to tear down the house that instant. They had brought a bulldozer . . . I remember thinking that it was a huge toy. I had never seen anything like it. I was extremely happy with the bulldozer until I saw the fear on my mother's face and the way she was hurriedly putting things together to take with us. She thought they were going to tear the house down on top of us. At that time there was a fear of federal authorities that does not exist today. I remember vividly that many Puerto Ricans, including Viequenses, believed that the penalty for a violation of federal law was imprisonment in Atlanta. . . . I remember looking back and being fascinated as the bulldozer tore down our home. My mother, on the other hand, was crying, not knowing where to go. (p. 51)

JUSTIFICATION FOR MILITARY PRESENCE

U.S. involvement with various wars justified its military presence in Vieques. Historically, World War II, the Cuban Missile Crisis, the Cold War, the war against the spread of communism, and the need to protect the Venezuelan oil fields and Saudi Arabia's oil tankers, were used to rectify the need for military training in Puerto Rico. Other historical events were:

the overthrow of Guatemalan President in 1954, the Cuban Bay of Pigs operation in 1961, the invasion of the Dominican Republic in 1965, the overthrow of Chilean President Salvador Allende in 1973, the invasion of Grenada in 1983, and the invasion of Panama in 1989, . . . to train the Contras fighting Nicaragua's Sandinista government, . . . members of El Salvador's armed forces in their war against the Farabundo Marti National Liberation Front . . . stopover for the British Royal Navy in the 1982 Malvinas/Falklands War . . . (1990s) to prepare for the war in the Persian Gulf. (Barreto, 2002, pp. 27-28)

After 9/11, the U.S. Navy sought to secure its presence in Vieques for training against terrorism. More recently, it trained for the invasion of

Iraq (Mullenneaux, 2000, p. 3). Ironically, mainly self-serving, the U.S. Navy trained to protect its empire by subjugating the rights, land, and the ecosystem of the Viequenses. Yet, Viequenses lacked local police protection from those U.S. servicemen that solicited prostitutes, harassed the local women and girls, and perpetrated violent criminal acts while intoxicated (Barreto, 2002, p. 29; Mullenneaux, 2000, p. 30).

The War on Drugs became another reason for upholding the U.S. Navy in Vieques. Thus far, the military presence has not curtailed the trafficking of narcotics to the U.S., nor has any protection been offered to the thousands of missing Latin American women and children exploited by the lucrative black market of prostitution and pornography (Twohey, 2000; Watts & Zimmerman, 2002).

Political Tactics

Puerto Rico's political ideologies, especially of the conservative side, have also confused, distorted and repressed those Puerto Ricans involved in the struggle for social and economic justice. Since 1940, protests against the atrocities committed by the military have existed. However, any anti-American movement was perceived as a threat to the existing political, social and economic ties with the U.S. According to this conscious or unconscious belief, anti-military movements were seen as tactics used by leftist militant partisans in favor of Puerto Rico's independence from the U.S. Leftist radicals have historically been labeled as communist, and/or terrorist. As a consequence, many Puerto Ricans were led to believe the myth that any support toward demilitarization was anti-American, therefore jeopardizing any designated federal funds (Barreto, 2000, p. 48) In reality, the use of such a repressive tactic would boomerang and dent the U.S. markets.

> About 70% of the net domestic income generated in Puerto Rico leaves the island . . . (O)ne-third of the total value of the productive activity in Puerto Rico turns into payments that the residents of Puerto Rico never see. The net U.S. government transfers–$8,315 million in 1999, most of them vested rights of the people as Social Security or Veterans Pensions–pale when compared to earnings remissions toward the U.S. for $21,717 million in the same year. This comparison does not take into consideration that U.S. military forces in Puerto Rico do not pay rent for the bases and the 12% of the land it occupies. (Committee for Human Rights in Puerto Rico, 2000, p. 146-147)

In addition, the U.S. Navy made $80 million a year for renting Vieques to other foreign countries for their military maneuvers (McCafferty, 2002, p. 6).

DEMILITARIZATION

The fear of being ostracized, discriminated against or classified as terrorist restricted most anti-military movements. On April 19, 1999, however, the death of a civilian security guard for the Navy, David Sanes Rodríguez underscored the myth of the U.S. Navy's protective role. As noted by Mullenneaux (2000),

> the Navy's 'shooting script' went disastrously awry . . . the pilot of a FA-18C Hornet flying at 400 miles an hour was cleared to drop two Mark-82 500-pound bombs . . . payload missed its target by a mile and a half, killing a civilian security guard and injuring four others. Nothing in the bomb run, it turned out, went according to plan. And it would change the Navy's relationship with Vieques forever. (p. 13)

It also changed the views Puerto Ricans held of the Navy. The people of Puerto Rico realized that the Navy was as destructive as any terrorist attack and as oppressive as any military regime. The Puerto Rican community retaliated by dropping a heavier bomb. It dropped its fears, stereotypes, and self-doubts. This explosion produced a sense of solidarity, empowering the Puerto Rican people in the island and mainland to fight for human rights, social justice, and self-determination (Barreto, 2002). Social and radical activists in the Vieques movement were empowered to continue their efforts in organizing and networking with committed support groups in Puerto Rico and the U.S. (McCaffrey, 1998). No longer did the relationship with the U.S. and the Navy prove divisive between the various conservative, status quo and/or pro-statehood political parties. It was a human justice matter and a common cause, bonding Puerto Ricans in the island with those in the mainland.

The violation of human rights captured world attention. By June 1999, both the Governor of Puerto Rico and President Clinton appointed two separate committees to study the Navy's impact in Vieques. By the end of the year, President Clinton recommended for the Navy to sustain its training for the next five years and offered an economic incentive of $40 million to Puerto Rico. The governor of Puerto Rico did not accept President Clinton's offer but agreed with the White House to have Viequenses vote on the demilitarization of Vieques (Mullenneaux, 2000, p. 9-12). Neither the Viequenses nor the community-at-large accepted the Rosselló-Clinton agreement; much less the continuation of bombing with inept weapons. Protesters were met with pepper spray and tear gas by the riot squad and police. However, many activists called for a nonviolent civil disobedience and took bullhorns to remind 'people to stay calm' (McCaffrey, 2002, p. 171). The protesters remained resilient and committed to nonviolence during the Vieques crisis.

Ecology and Health

The impact of the U.S. Navy on the ecology of Vieques also captured great attention. Since 1947, the Navy used napalm, depleted uranium, carcinogens and other toxic substances at levels that violated the Pentagon's regulations (Murillo, 2001,p. 60). Elevated levels of several contaminants have impacted the water, food chain, and land. "The USS Killen, a destroyer used as a target ship during nuclear tests in the Marshall Islands, lies sunk 150 yards from shore" (Brown, 2003, retrieved 10/26/03). "Between 1983 and 1998, the Navy dropped 17,783 tons of bombs on Vieques" (Berman Santana, 2002, p. 41). William Risley (2002), a consultant to Analytical Research Laboratories, found a patient from Vieques to have the worst toxic and mineral level ever noted in the laboratory. Studies conducted by the Puerto Rico Health Department found that compared to Puerto Rico, Vieques had a higher rate of cancer, asthma, diabetes, hypertension (Roman, 2003; EFE World News Service, 2003), infant mortality, (Berman Santana, 2002) and mental illness (Business Wire, 1999). Some environment advisors consider that the U.S. Navy violated a number of federal laws, i.e., Endangered Species Act, the Clean Water Act, the Clean Air Act, etc. (Inter Press Service, 1999). By the end of 1999, at least 55 Vieques cancer patients and landowners had filed a $109 million class-action suit against the Navy (Mullenneaux, 2000, p. 12).

Solidarity Through Nonviolent Civil Disobedience

The awareness and consciousness-raising planted for the struggle for human and environmental rights finally blossomed to full force. The Vieques crisis flourished into a united front, mobilizing people from different political parties, religious groups, artists and leaders from other countries. In contrast to previous anti-military movements, no buyouts or repressive threats of cutting federal education funds could regulate this movement (Barreto, pp. 56-57, 69). Over 150,000 people attended the Peace for Vieques March in San Juan, Puerto Rico, on February 21, 2000 (Mullenneaux, 2000, p.12). Other rallies were held in

New York City and the 2000 Democratic Convention in Los Angeles. Attracting worldwide attention, neither spectators nor U.S. politicians could ignore, deny or avoid the Vieques situation.

> Regular efforts to educate and lobby Congress include a visit by hundreds of Viequenses and Puerto Ricans to Washington, D.C., during March 2001, when some legislators expressed surprise that Vieques was inhabited! By far the most powerful activism has been militant, nonviolent civil disobedience . . . within a year, 14 protest camps had been established, representing teachers, fishermen, church groups and others. (Berman Santana, 2002, p. 43)

Washington, D.C., became the national headquarters for the Vieques Support Network. Supported by the Puerto Rican Solidarity Committee, it linked various support groups from New York City, Philadelphia, Chicago, and other cities in the U.S. (McCaffrey, 1998; Mullenneaux, 2000).

Viequenses spearheaded the Committee for the Rescue and Development of Vieques (CRPDV) whose purpose was to achieve the Four Ds: Demilitarization, Decontamination, Devolution (return of all Navy land to Viequenses), and Economic Development (Mullenneaux, 2000, p. 8). In support of nonviolent protests, CRPDV provided resources to protest campers. Teachers from the Puerto Rican Federation of Teachers provided literature on civil disobedience. Attorneys from the Puerto Rican Bar Association taught campers their constitutional rights and provided free legal assistant to any camper arrested for trespassing. If arrested, leftist political leaders (e.g., Rubén Berríos) and lawyers advised the protesters to not resist arrest, and to go in a peaceful and civil manner. Even the far right pro statehood politicians in power "suggested the legislature hold all its sessions in the Navy's live-fire zone if the military refused to back down" (Mullenneaux, 2000, p. 74).

It is not clear if the 1979 death of Angel Rodríguez Cristóbal was seminal to this nonviolent civil disobedience. Angel Rodríguez Cristóbal was one of 150 demonstrators that trespassed into Navy waters and territory. On May 19, 1979, Angel Rodríguez Cristóbal became one of the 21 protestors arrested by federal marshals during an ecumenical service in Vieques. Although the army of federal marshals intended to break-up the Vieques movement, the press captured the marshals' repressive tactics used during the arrests. Known as the "Vieques 21," Angel Rodríguez Cristóbal, along with eleven others, was fined $500.00 and sentenced to serve six months in federal prison. Two months into his term, Angel Rodríguez Cristóbal was found dead at the Tallahassee

Federal Institution. U.S. authorities declared his death a suicide while friends and family claimed otherwise. Independent autopsy and photos of the cadaver showed severe beatings and inconsistencies to suicide by strangulation (McCaffrey, 2002, p. 90). Some suggested that he was assassinated and his death a repressive message to other activists in Vieques (Murillo, 2001, p. 49). In retaliation to his mysterious death, "the Macheteros (Machete Wielders), a revolutionary pro-independence organization attacked a navy bus, killing two servicemen" (Barreto, p. 31). Murillo (2001) noted that *ABC News* correspondent Bill Greenwood described this event as a "confrontation between Navy officials and terrorists" (p. 49). As previously discussed, such a misnomer serves to regulate any social anti-military movement in place. Finally, after a two decade span between the deaths of Angel Rodríguez Cristóbal (1979) and David Sanes Rodríguez (1999), the people of Puerto Rico were clear that only a nonpartisan approach would maintain the united front in the struggle for human and ecological rights of the Viequenses.

It can also be argued that the strong presence of the religious sector influenced the call for peace and nonviolent behavior. A coalition of ministers, nuns, bishops and the Puerto Rican Bible Society clearly demonstrated their opposition of the Navy in Vieques (The Christian Century, 2003; Mullenneaux, 2000). It was evident that neither protesters nor the Navy could afford to confront each other in front of a vigilant worldwide audience. Greater caution occurred during the arrests of Reverend Al Sharpton, Rev. Jesse Jackson's wife Jackie Jackson, James Edward Olmos, and Robert Kennedy, Jr. This civil disobedient and peaceful movement inspired Guatemalan Peace Nobel Prize laureate Rigoberta Menchu, the Dalai Lama, Rev. Jesse Jackson, and Mayor Giuliani to visit Vieques and join the struggle for social justice and the demilitarization of Vieques. The movement flourished as the national media captured the visits of presidential candidate Al Gore. It has been suggested that New York candidates supported the demilitarization in Vieques in order to gain votes from the Puerto Rican community. Quite impressive was NY State Senator Hillary Rodman Clinton's visit to Vieques during her campaign. Yet, some did recall when as First Lady, Hillary Rodman Clinton did not support President Clinton's humanitarian action of granting clemency to the Puerto Rican activists imprisoned in 1979 (see section on Angel Rodríguez Cristóbal, page 14). Republican candidate for re-election, New York State governor George Pataki called for the bombing to stop during his high profiled visit. In a similar fashion, the AFL-CIO, world known entertainers (i.e., Ricky Martin,

Rosie Pérez), world-boxing champions (i.e., Felix 'Tito' Trinidad and José 'Chegui' Torres), and Miss Universe (Denise Quiñones) became conduits for peace in Vieques (Barreto, 2000). Their positions demonstrated to the world the Puerto Rican people's camaraderie against the U.S. Navy. Since May 2000, more than 2000 people had participated in acts of civil disobedience (Acevedo-Delgado, 2003).

The Struggle Continues

Finally, on June 14, 2001, President Bush reaffirmed former President Clinton's promise that the Navy would halt the military exercise and leave Vieques by May 2003. The U.S. government undermined the results of the July 2001 referendum where 70 percent of the residents in Vieques voted for an immediate end to military maneuvers (Hernández Betran, 2002). The last military maneuvers ended in February 2003. Unsurprisingly, the closing of the U.S. military base in Vieques on May 1, 2003 called for an island wide celebration. Viequenses and others rejoiced the ending of a 60-year-old battle.

Still in the hands of the federal government, the Navy transferred the property to the Department of Interior for developing a wildlife refuge. The U.S. Department of Fishing and Wildlife estimated $400 million would be needed to clean up the environmental mess, contamination, toxins, unexploded bombs, and other harmful toxic waste generated by military activities. In spite of the U.S. government intervention, Vieques is now a part of the *international* struggle against military activities that contaminate the global environment (Acevedo-Delgado, n.d.).

As previously noted, the health crisis still exists. With a high cancer mortality rate, a program was proposed that would provide transportation to those needing treatment to the Oncology Hospital at the Medical Center in Puerto Rico. A mobile unit for screening out cancer was also proposed. In spite of the Diagnostic and Treatment Center in Vieques, the health care reform and specialized services located outside of Vieques makes access to care somewhat difficult (Roman, May 10/03; Sosa, 2003). As Albor Ruiz (2003) reported, of the 9300 people in Vieques, 72% live below the poverty line and 50% are unemployed. Such figures only accentuate the welfare state of the Viequenses.

It is anticipated that the tourism industry would alleviate Vieques' economy. But, another environmental concern is the possible overflow of tourists invading the island. As the regional manager of the Puerto Rico Tourism Company reported: "They come in and ask if the water is safe to swim in . . . They want to see Camp Garcia . . . And they want real estate brochures" (Myers, 2003).

The Commonwealth of Puerto Rico will need to be vigilant of the powerful empire of the Hiltons, Hyatts, Marriotts, and other resort developers with U.S. corporate ties. To lose sight of those martyrs expropriated and forced to leave their homes would only pave the invasion of the new global colonizers.

CONCLUSIONS

Finally, after 60 years of military presence, Puerto Ricans in Puerto Rico and the mainland recognized how the U.S. Navy destroyed their people's lives, their beaches, environment, and livelihood. Awareness, consciousness-raising, solidarity, and civil disobedience were effective tools used in the struggle for achieving social, economic, and environmental justice for the people in Vieques. These tools served to overcome the repressive colonial tactics used by the U.S. Navy, maintain focus on the issue, and embrace Puerto Ricans in spite of political, religious, class, and geographical differences.

In essence, the bottom-up grassroots social movement relied on the reflection of the lives of those Viequenses historically oppressed by the U.S. Navy. The reflection of the people's lives served to deconstruct false ideologies used by the U.S. to restrict any anti-military movement. This social movement welcomed others of different creeds, cultures, political ideologies, social class, occupation, etc. Such openness empowered and energized the people in their struggle for social justice. The remains of this social movement provides the foresight for understanding that, in spite of this victory, the struggle for a national identity, democracy, and the protection of human and environmental rights will continue. It hopes that people from other sectors of the world also recognize that the U.S. *cultural* imperialism will not cease to gain control over indigenous cultures in these post-modern times (Ritzer, 1998, p. 87). Therefore, the Vieques experience must serve as a model of social change and be passed on to future generations. The solidarity of the Puerto Rican people must be glorified during each and every commemoration of their victory over the greatest naval force in the history of the world.

REFERENCES

Acevedo-Delgado, G. (n.d.) Vieques: After the navy left. *New World Look: The Mission Magazine of the United Methodist Church.* Retrieved February 14, 2004 from http://gbgm-umc.org/global_news/full_article.cfm?articlcid=1734

Barreto, A.A. (2002). *Vieques, the Navy and Puerto Rican politics.* Gainesville, FL: University Press of Florida.

Berman Santana, D. (2002, Spring-Summer). Resisting toxic militarism: Vieques versus the U.S. Navy. *Social Justice,* 37-48.

Brown, M.H. (2003, January 24). *Knight Ridder/Tribune News Service.* pK7106. Retrieved October 26, 2003, from InfoTrac OneFile, Electronic Collection: CJ96869135.

Committee for Human Rights in Puerto Rico (Sponsor). (2000, Winter). International tribunal on violation of human rights in Puerto Rico and Vieques by the United States of America. *Social Justice, 27*(4), 143-151.

Comprehensive behavioral health care study suggests link between military exercises, poor health status on Puerto Rican island of Vieques (1999, August 9). *Business Wire,* 1247.

Conway, D. (1998). Microstates in a macroworld. In T. Klak (Ed). *Globalization and Neoliberalsim: The Caribbean Context.* Lanham, MD: Rowman & Littlefield Publishers, Inc.

Dietz, J.L. (1986). *Economic history of Puerto Rico: Institutional change and capitalist development.* Princeton, NJ: Princeton University Press, Ch.3.

Hernández Beltran, R.E. (June 10, 2002). Puerto Ricans demand U.S. Navy's withdrawal from Vieques. *EFE World News Service,* Retrieved October 26, 2003, from InfoTrac OneFile, Electronic Collection: A87058680.

History Task Force, Center for Puerto Rican Studies (1979). *Labor migration under capitalism: The Puerto Rican experience.* New York: Monthly Review Press.

López, A. (1974). The beginnings of colonization: Puerto Rico, 1493-1800. In A. López, & J. Petras, (Eds.) *Puerto Rico and Puerto Ricans: Studies in history and society* (pp. 12-41). Cambridge, MA: Schenkman Publishing Co.

Jiménez de Wagenheim, O. (1997). *Puerto Rico's revolt for independence: El Grito de Lares.* Princeton, NJ: Markus Weiner Publishing, Inc.

Maldonado-Denis, M. (1972). *Puerto Rico: A socio-historic interpretation.* New York: Random House.

McCaffrey, K. (2002). *Military power and popular protest: The U.S. Navy in Vieques, Puerto Rico.* New Brunswick, NJ: Rutgers University Press.

McCaffrey, K. (1998). Forging solidarity: Politics, protest, and the Vieques solidarity network. In A. Torres & J.E. Velázquez (Eds.), *The Puerto Rican movement: Voices from the diaspora.* Philadelphia, PA: Temple University Press.

Mullenneaux, L. (2000). *¡Ni una bomba más! Vieques vs. U.S. Navy* (2nd ed.). New York, NY: The Penington Press.

Murillo, M. (2001). *Islands of resistance: Puerto Rico, Vieques, and U.S. policy.* New York, NY: Seven Stories Press.

Myers, G.N. (2003, June 16). Vieques: Quiet isle or tourism target? *Travel Weekly,* 62 (24), Electronic Collection: A104440578.

Nieves-Falcón, L. (1975). *El emigrante de puertorriqueño.* Río Piedras, PR: Editorial Edil, Inc.

Padrón, H. 1989. *The history and culture of Puerto Rico*. Rochester, NY: The City School District.

Rabin, R. (n.d.) Vieques: Five centuries of struggle and resistance. In *Historia de Vieques, Puerto Rico, Vieques Historical Archives*. Retrieved February 14, 2003 from http://www.vieques-island.com/navy/

Ramírez de Arellano, A.B. & Seipp, C. (1983). *Colonialism, Catholicism and contraception: A history of birth control in Puerto Rico*. Chapel Hill, NC: The University of North Carolina.

Ribes Tobar, F. (1973). *A chronological history of Puerto Rico*. New York, NY: Educational Publishers, Inc.

Rights-Puerto Rico: Environmental tragedy in Vieques. (1999, June 15). *Inter Press Service*, p1008165w005.

Risely, W. (2002, March). Vieques, Puerto Rico . . . is the problem deeper than we think? *Original Internist, 9* (1), 27-29.

Ritzer, G. (1998). *The McDonaldization thesis: Explorations and extensions*. Thousand Oaks, CA: Sage Publications, Inc.

Roman, I. (2003, May 10). Study: Vieques' cancer rates higher than Puerto Rico. *Knight Ridder/Tribune News Service*, pk0258. Retrieved September 1, 2003, from InfoTrac OneFile, Article CJ101540622.

Roman, I. (2003, May 1). U.S. Navy exits Vieques, Puerto Rico, bombing ranges; Cleanup becomes priority. *Knight Ridder/Tribune Business News*, pITEM03121035. Retrieved October 26, 2003, from InfoTrac OneFile, Electronic Collection: CJ100995623.

Ruiz, A. (2003, November 23) Navy must clean up its Vieques mess. *Puerto Rico Herald*. Retrieved February 19, 2003 from http://www.puertorico-herald.org/issues/2004/vol8n06/NavyMustClean.shtml

Silén, J.A. (1971). *We the Puerto Rican people: A story of oppression and resistance*. London, E.C. 1: Monthly Review Press.

Sosa, O. (2003, May 10). Promesas de más servicios oncológicos. *El Nuevo Día Interactivo*, Retrieved February 14, 2004 from http://www.endi.com/archivo/vieques/noticias.asp?newsid=29787

The Christian Century Foundation, (2003, March 22). Activist hail Navy plan to leave Vieques. *The Christian Century, 120* (6), 15.

Twohey, M. (2000, May 20). Faith and feminism fight sexual slavery. *National Journal, 32* (21), 1626.

Vieques residents seek compensation from U.S. Navy (2003, September 24). *EFE World News Service*. Retrieved October 22, 2003 from http://webpac.brockport.edu:2067/itw/infomark/788/457/37916727w7/purl=rc1_ITOF_0

Yellow Bird, M. (2001). Critical values and First Nations Peoples. In R. Fong and S. Furuto (Eds.), *Culturally competent practice: Skills, interventions and evaluation* (pp. 61-74). Needham Heights, MA: Allyn & Bacon.

Watts, C. & Zimmerman, C. (2002, April 6). Violence against women: Global scope and magnitude. *The Lancet, 359* (9313), 1232.

Dónde Están los Huevos? Surviving in Times of Economic Hardship: Cuban Mothers, the State, and Making Ends Meet

Rebecca Burwell

SUMMARY. Since the collapse of the Soviet Union in the late 1980s, Cuba has experienced difficult economic times. This paper examines the survival strategies that Cuban women have developed for making ends meet. Through working in the dollar economy and using extensive household networks of support, Cuban mothers are able to negotiate the demands of being both caregivers and wage earners. Furthermore, Cuban women's partnership with the state and the Cuban state's assistance to its citizens in the form of subsidized child care, education, health care, housing, and food enables households to survive despite difficult economic times, unlike the trends in the privatization in state services, seen elsewhere in Latin America. *[Article copies available for a fee from The Haworth Document Delivery Service: 1-800-HAWORTH. E-mail address: <docdelivery@haworthpress.com> Website: <http://www.HaworthPress.com> © 2004 by The Haworth Press, Inc. All rights reserved.]*

Rebecca Burwell, PhD, is Research Associate at the Center for the Study of Latino Religion, University of Notre Dame, South Bend, Indiana. She wishes to thank Dr. Judith Wittner, Dr. Maria Vidal de Haymes, Dr. Marilyn Krogh, and Dr. Richard Dello Buono for their help in preparing this chapter.

[Haworth co-indexing entry note]: "Dónde Están los Huevos? Surviving in Times of Economic Hardship: Cuban Mothers, the State, and Making Ends Meet." Burwell, Rebecca. Co-published simultaneously in *Journal of Poverty* (The Haworth Press, Inc.) Vol. 8, No. 4, 2004, pp. 75-95; and: *Poverty and Inequality in the Latin American-U.S. Borderlands: Implications of U.S. Interventions* (ed: Keith M. Kilty, and Elizabeth A. Segal) The Haworth Press, Inc., 2004, pp. 75-95. Single or multiple copies of this article are available for a fee from The Haworth Document Delivery Service [1-800-HAWORTH, 9:00 a.m. - 5:00 p.m. (EST). E-mail address: docdelivery@haworthpress.com].

http://www.haworthpress.com/web/JPOV
Digital Object Identifier: 10.1300/J134v08n04_05

KEYWORDS. Women, Cuba, poverty, survival strategies, state-centered development

INTRODUCTION: SURVIVAL IN CUBA

Havana, Cuba, November, 2001.

> *While we carried our groceries back from the dollar store, people began staring at us as we made our way into our building. At first, I wasn't sure what made our neighbors take such an interest in us. It couldn't be the sight of two "yanquis" carrying large bags; people knew us in the neighborhood, our mere presence didn't necessarily merit raised eyebrows at that point. After a moment, I realized that it was the big box that I carried, gingerly balanced in my arms: a crate of 3 dozen eggs, one of the most precious and sought-after food items in Cuba at the time. We had bought the eggs at the dollar grocery store, one of the biggest and most well-stocked stores in Havana, located in the wealthier, embassy neighborhood called Miramar.*
>
> *The unavailability of eggs provoked the most oft asked question in the autumn months of 2001: "Dónde están los huevos?" or "Where're the eggs?" After a few more moments of staring, as if on cue, an older Cuban woman with a brown flowered dress and dyed reddish hair sitting on the front steps yelled out, "Where'd you find those eggs?" (Fieldnotes, 2001)*

While conducting my dissertation research in 2001, conversation topics such as finding food, economic hardship, and making ends meet permeated everyday talk with people in Cuba, from serious discussion to neighborly chitchat in the streets. For a growing number of the world's population, physical survival organizes daily life, from finding food, to feeding one's children, to discovering means by which money can be made to pay for tomorrow's dinner. It is also a gendered struggle, one in which women take on much of the responsibility for providing for other people, through feeding, clothing, and caring for them.

Since the collapse of the Soviet Union in the late 1980s, Cuba has experienced economic insecurity, much of which was being alleviated during the time that I was there conducting research. The survival strategies that Cuban women developed for making ends meet often facilitated or at least sustained a sense of "we-ness" between Cubans, meaning that sharing and swapping resources were commonplace and referred to often as a cultural practice, part of a national ethic and identity. This reciprocity has created relationships of obligation across households, between neighbors, co-workers, and kin. In this article, I discuss Cuban women's strategies for making ends meet, their partnership with the state, and how the Cuban state's assistance to people, in the form of subsidized child care, education, health care, housing, and food enables households to survive despite difficult economic times.

From 2000 to 2003, I took four trips to Cuba where I conducted 48 face-to-face interviews and fieldwork with Cuban women ages 18 to 72 for my dissertation. I used a life history approach with the women I interviewed, touching on such topics as childhood, education, family life, and their day-to-day tasks. In the interviews, I explored how Cuban mothers make ends meet in a time of economic crisis and how Cubans have survived food shortages, energy crises, and economic instability. I also wanted to understand the role of the Cuban state in providing assistance to its citizens, through nationalized healthcare, a monthly ration of food, subsidized housing, free education, and subsidized childcare.

FOOD, THE REVOLUTION, THE "SPECIAL PERIOD," AND THE EMBARGO

The search for food, hunger, and economic survival are international problems that much of the world experiences (Harriss-White and Hoffenberg, 1994; DeRose, Messer, and Millman, 1998). Although these issues occur in almost all parts of the world, food shortages, lack of good medical care, medicine, malnutrition, substandard housing, and few economic resources are everyday occurrences for the majority of people living in developing countries.

In Cuba, many of these problems have been addressed by the Cuban state's provision of universal healthcare, education, and monthly food rations. However, in spite of this support, difficult economic times have forced Cubans to find other ways to supplement the state's support. In order to buy a variety of food products and not be limited by the ration card, Cubans must possess dollars. This search for dollars organizes daily life for the majority of Cubans. For example, every citizen receives a monthly ration of basic foodstuffs, known as the *libreta*, a small notebook that records how much rice, oil, chicken, milk, beans, and vegetables to which each family/individual is entitled (Benjamin,

Collins, and Scott, 1984). However, there are still problems with food shortages, and women complain that their monthly food rations run out before the month ends. Women, who perform most of the domestic and reproductive labor in Cuba, feel these food shortages most acutely, as they search for creative ways to feed their families.

Before the advent of the revolution in Cuba in 1959, food shortages and poverty were widespread, with 30-40% of the urban population and 60% of the rural population experiencing hunger and malnutrition. In addition, about the richest 20% of the population received more than 55% of the national income, while the poorest 20% received between 2% and 6% of the national income. Likewise, 9% of the landowners owned 62% of the land, while the bottom 66% of farm workers owned 7% of the land. To address these inequities, a few of the goals of the revolution included the redistribution of land, the provision of health care for the population, and the supplementing of diets such that hunger would be eradicated. Now, Cuba has health indicators that rival First World countries, a high rate of literacy, and a well-developed education system. With the triumph of the revolution and support from the Soviet Union, many of the goals of providing health care, nutrition, and education for the population had been achieved.

Although Cuba has far fewer food problems than most other Latin American or Caribbean countries, it still periodically faces food crises and endured a devastating blow to its economy and food supplies after the fall of the communist bloc. In 1989, after the collapse of the Soviet Union, malnutrition and food scarcity increased. By 1992, President Boris Yeltsin had called an end to all economic assistance. Cuba's major export crop, sugar, could not sustain the economy, and the Cuban State was forced to find other ways to increase the GNP as well as feed its population. The early 1990s were years of "shared scarcity" and President Castro called the period, "The Special Period in the Time of Peace."

Before the Special Period, the majority of the Cuban diet had come from food imports, but Cuba lost 70% of its imports when the Soviet Union collapsed. The food shortages devastated much of the population. Meat disappeared from markets, many basic products were returned to the ration system, and some supplies of staple items, such as beans and rice, became very unstable (Frank and Reed, 1997).

In addition, Cuba continued to be devastated by the U.S. embargo, which has created economic losses for Cuba of about $60 billion and which has isolated Cuba from many of the world's much needed food and fuel resources (Schwab, 1999). The Cuban Democracy Act, signed by President Bush in 1992, not only continued the economic war against Cuba, but also forced U.S. subsidiaries trading with Cuba to curtail their trade activities through a variety of sanctions. For instance, the U.S. embargo prevents U.S. subsidiaries from trading or selling products made with Cuban parts. Consequently, the embargo blocks not only U.S. companies' trade with Cuba, but has choked other countries' trade relations with Cuba, further devastating the Cuban people.

To address this crisis, the Cuban government introduced a number of measures to generate income and increase the GNP. In 1993, the Cuban state legalized the dollar economy, creating a dual economic system: *pesos*, which is the Cuban currency and U.S. dollars. Most Cubans work for the state and therefore are paid in pesos. However, Cuba has developed relations with non-U.S. multinational corporations that invested in joint state-private ventures, and has opened up the island to the tourist industry. Many of these industries, particularly the tourist industry are part of the dollar economy. Tourists must pay in dollars to stay in the hotels, eat in restaurants, and enjoy Cuban entertainment. Bringing dollars into the economy has enabled the state to increase its hard currency. Consequently, the government could buy much needed fuel, fertilizers, and food products, and could increase their GNP in order to recover from the Special Period.

Presently, the economy and everyday life has returned to some semblance of normalcy. Cubans still experience some effects of the economic crisis of the Special Period. For example, the state still rations some food products, such as eggs or meat. The economic crisis of the 1990s has also exacerbated pre-existing social inequalities. Now that there is a dual economy, possessing dollars means that some families can buy more, since many rationed items such as chicken or milk are sold in dollars in the dollar stores. Anyone in Cuba has access to the dollar stores, but one can only use U.S. dollars to buy the groceries, clothing, or personal products that these stores sell. Although there are other stores that sell these products in *pesos*, the dollar stores tend to have better products, more variety, and are well stocked with goods that are often rationed or not sold in *peso* stores.

Despite the strides made by the state, life is still difficult in Cuba. In the fall of 2001, Cuba's tourist industry declined, due to the terrorist attacks in New York on September 11th and the decrease worldwide in international travel. Then in November, Hurricane Michelle struck the island, which further devastated Cuba's agricultural base, resulting in further shortages of fuel and basic food items. Although the state did a noteworthy job in evacuating communities, preparing people for the energy losses, and providing food and water for marginalized communities during the hurricane, the government could not prevent all of the economic losses that the storm left in its wake.

Although everyday life did not devolve into the chaos that many would predict after the hurricane and the loss in the tourist trade, it did affect people's lives. This included waiting in longer lines for the buses, due to a lack of fuel, and searching daily for certain food products whose supply was unstable, such as eggs and meat. My friend Daniel, a 28 year old engineer stated one day as we waited in a long bus line for a short ride to a friend's house, *"There's tension in the air . . . people are worried. I am afraid of what might happen"* (Fieldnotes, 2001).

In addition, two more hurricanes pummeled Cuba in the fall of 2002, causing more agricultural losses. The spring of 2003 was also difficult for Cubans, as the advent of the Iraq war and the escalation of tensions between the U.S. and Cuba made Cubans fearful of the future.

While all Cubans endure many difficulties, women tend to be the ones that shoulder the primary responsibility of maintaining home life, as well as providing economically for their families (Catasus-Cervera, 1996). Even though the state has institutionalized a Family Code in 1975 that states that men and women are equals and should share equally in family and domestic duties, in practice, women still assume much of the responsibility for caring for children and the elderly.

The change over to a dual economy and the recovery from the Special Period have made providing for one's family a more time-consuming task. Consequently, women often must develop strategies for making ends meet when state pensions and salaries don't stretch far enough and when some material resources are only available in dollars or not obtainable on the regulated, legal market. Thus, the women I interviewed named strategies that they utilized for surviving, both in economic terms, and in terms of being able to simultaneously be care-givers and wage-earners. These strategies include: working in the street, utilizing extensive household networks for support, receiving money from transnational family relations, and employing assistance from the state.

SURVIVING AND MAKING ENDS MEET

Working in the Street

About 40% of women who are mothers in Cuba work for pay outside of the home (Suarez, 1998). This statistic is based on the number of women who work for the state; however, with the introduction of dollars into the Cuban economy in the early 1990s, many more women also work in what they call "the street." This does not connote prostitution, as usually understood in the U.S. and other places. For women in Cuba, "working in the street" means selling food, selling toys/small utensils/other products for dollars, bartering one's services for other services (i.e., offering to give someone a pedicure in exchange for a haircut), renting a room, or even cooking food for tourists or students.

When women refer to working in the street, they are not talking about *legal* activity undertaken to secure dollars; they are referring to basic "hustling"–selling goods or services in order to secure a few dollars. While some women do work for foreign companies and are taxed by the Cuban state, when women describe what they do as "working in the street," they are referring to *unregulated* economic activity, undertaken solely to secure dollars. They are selling items or performing services for dollars that they do not report to the state. This includes women selling scarce goods that family members send to them from the U.S. or elsewhere, such as make-up, running shoes, or children's toys, objects that are usually only sold for dollars, but sold in amounts that are too expensive for most Cubans to obtain. Thus, they are sold on the street for less money, but still for dollars.

One mother I interviewed, 35 year old Ana, lives in Lawton, one of the poorer areas of Havana, far removed from the central tourist and business district. She lives in an apartment above her uncles and grandmother's house. There are 8 people in the household, which includes her 9-year-old daughter. The upstairs rooms, which had been built onto the flat-roofed, concrete square house, include a kitchen, living room and two bedrooms. She shares a bedroom with her husband and daughter while her two nieces sleep in the next room.

Ana had worked as a teacher in a *círculo* (day care center), but as a single mother, she quit her job, and therefore could not make ends meet (she subsequently remarried, but her husband was out of work as well). Although she receives a subsidy from the state, she has begun a pedicure/manicure business in her home, where for a few dollars, she does her neighbors' nails. She describes her work as "working in the street" since it is not regulated by the state and since it is solely for the purpose of hustling for dollars. When I asked her why she got involved in this work, she said:

> I didn't study. I worked in the *círculos*. But, I have been one year without a job. Now, I work in the street . . . it costs less to work in

the home. I don't have transportation worries. I can spend the time I need finding food. At one time I worked in a *fábrica* (factory) as a line worker. Everyday my back and arms were sore. Now, people come to my house. My family helps me, too. Before, I made $180 pesos a month ($8 U.S. dollars). Now, I can make more, doing hair and painting nails (Personal Interview, November, 2001).

Similarly, Paula, a 34-year-old single mother with an eight-year-old daughter, suffers from severe depression and therefore is not able to work. She survives on a small subsidy, a disability payment from the state that amounts to about 150 pesos or 8 U.S. dollars a month. However, this is not enough on which to survive. Paula, told me, "I sell baked goods in the street, guava bread or bananas for a good price . . . my sister and brother help me, too" (Personal Interview, November, 2001). In addition, she sells paintings that she buys from a Cuban artist who is one of her friends. Paula buys the artwork for a low price in pesos and then turns around and sells the paintings in dollars to tourists in the street. In fact, this is how I met her, as she tried to sell me paintings of brightly painted landscapes, promising a "good price," done by a Cuban artist.

Finally, one of my informants, a young single mother, Berta, who lives in Marianao, a western section of Havana, described her work as "working in the street." She sells clothes that she gets from her family living outside of Cuba or her baby's father. She said:

> I am a housewife . . . I worked cleaning in a hospital. But, things are difficult now, these are bad economic times, the salaries are low. I work in the street, selling clothes. There is more liberty that way. It's not too difficult, but it is always a struggle, *la lucha*, to find food. I look for food in the afternoon, but since I don't work, she (her daughter) can't go to the *círculo*, so my mother watches her while I look for food. (Personal Interview, December, 2001)

Many women who are professionals do have some way to access dollars in a legal manner. For example, one university professor, Theresa, a petite, divorced, 40-year-old woman whom I interviewed, spends at least one month a year helping to develop an exchange program between a university in Great Britain and the University of Havana. She is paid in dollars by the university in Great Britain to work with them; she then has to pay a tax to the Cuban state on her "dollar wages." Thus, she is able to make ends meet through legally recognized, taxable work that allows her to have dollars but that also is regulated by the state. When visiting her home one night, she pointed out all the new appliances she had been able to buy. She said:

> I think that sink (in the bathroom) I got after I worked in Brazil. It is hard to get these materials in Cuba. I also got the refrigerator after I had been working in London. Most of this stuff I got working elsewhere. (Personal Interview, November, 2001)

Likewise, Sylvia, a separated, 35-year-old physicist who works for a state-run pharmaceutical lab, had done some work in Belgium, working with a French pharmaceutical company, developing a drug to be sold in Europe. She was paid as a consultant, and that money, while again taxed by the Cuban state, was paid in dollars. When I asked about her experience in Belgium and why she went there, she said,

> It affected my son a lot, the separation . . . the financial times make it difficult . . . but my son does not lack for anything. (Personal Interview, November, 2001)

Women (and men) who have this sort of arrangement–the ability to work with non-Cuban organizations, schools, or businesses–are able to earn a decent income in a few months, an amount that would take them five or six years to earn in Cuba. An average Cuban salary is 350 pesos, or about 18 U.S. dollars a month, even for professional workers. Those who earn minimum wage earn roughly 100 pesos a month, or five U.S. dollars. Consequently, someone who earns between $500-1000 teaching or doing consulting for a foreign firm, while they might be taxed at high rate - sometimes 50%–they still take home more money working for a foreign company than they would ever make in a year in pesos, working for the state.

Thus, what is essential for survival in Cuba is to have access to dollars, either through legal, state regulated activity or through working in the street. However, since most women do not work in jobs where they have access to or opportunities for international work, they make do with selling goods or doing other types of work in the street. While I did not encounter any women in my research who engaged in prostitution, this is also a highly paid, lucrative business for young women, who connect with foreign business men and are paid in dollars for their services.

Multigenerational Family Help

Few families in Havana live in nuclear family households, due to a shortage in housing. It is more likely that a family will live in a nuclear unit in rural areas or small towns; however, in Havana, few households only consist of parents or children or married, childless couples (Smith and Padula, 1996). In my research, only about 20% of the respondents lived in nuclear family units.

Sharing housing is an important strategy for making ends meet because it allows women to more easily share resources, child care, and/or work in the street. In addition, multi-generational, overcrowded households means negotiating the many demands of an intergenerational household: caring for elderly parents, living with adult children, watching grandchildren, all of which has produced family tensions and other problems. However, these living situations have also provided much needed support for women. Much of the housing problem in Cuba is due to a lack of material resources, such as concrete and paint, which has been worsened by the U.S. embargo. The problems associated with the lack of safe, stable, and affordable housing are just a few of the problems related to the embargo.

Living in a multigenerational household, with more than 2-3 adult workers, means that between the adults, at least one person has the time or ability to work in the unregulated market or watch children or wait in line for scarce goods that appear haphazardly on the market. It also means that there are more workers available to barter for scarce goods, share childcare, and divide up household chores.

In some instances, the lack of housing and the increase in multigenerational households has been beneficial to families with young children. With more adults in the household, there is a more efficient sharing of resources and child-care duties. For example, in 1993, Theresa, a university professor and her two small sons, a one-year-old and 7-year-old, lived with her mother-in-law and her mother-in-law's parents, even though Theresa was divorced from her children's father. The difficult housing situation in addition to the stresses of being a single parent made it impossible for Theresa to find housing for just herself and her two children. Thus, living with her ex in-laws in a four generational household was the only solution. Theresa says:

> I have lived alone with them (my children) for three years. I got divorced in 1991, and following the divorce I started to live with my in-laws, until 1997. And, we also lived with my ex's grandparents,

this was all in a small apartment with four rooms, and the grandparents were really old and could not handle the conduct of young children. So, finally, after a few years, their father, had an apartment that had more rooms, and the *viejos* moved in with him.

Interviewer R: Why did all of those people live with you?

T: Well, the great-grandparents started to need help with daily life–there are groups in Cuban society that are vulnerable–children and old people. And, my ex-husband is an only child. So, I was the one to help out. (Personal Interview, November, 2001)

Between these different groups, then, usually someone has access to dollars or is not employed and therefore able to take care of the home, parents or children. In addition, there might be someone marginally employed, that is, they have flexible hours and can meet children after school or run household errands. Even though the economic problems brought about by the Special Period has meant that men have been more involved in the home, women still shoulder the majority of daily care-giving and domestic tasks in the household. In this case, Theresa did this negotiation and care for her ex-husband's family out of both her own needs (for housing) and their needs (for care), but also because the majority of care-work is work that is performed by women.

In another example, Olivia, a single, childless, retired nurse in her early 70s lives with her 68 year old sister, Elisabeth, Elisabeth's daughter and her husband, one teenage granddaughter, and two small children. Everyone except for Olivia and the children is employed. Thus, Olivia often brings the children to school in the morning and picks them up at 4 pm. She also helps with the feeding and playing with the children in the household.

Olivia usually runs errands to the *bodega* (the state run Cuban food store where people go each month to get their ration of rice, beans, sugar, etc.). She is the person designated to wait in line for scarce goods, like eggs, that might only come into the stores once in a while. One afternoon when I was at their house, Olivia comforted her niece Julia's newborn baby while Julia cooked. She also was helping to potty-train Tania, Julia's three-year-old daughter.

I asked Olivia what she did that day. She said that she went to the store in the morning, to find bread, eggs, or other things in *el shopping* (the dollar stores). Since she knew I would be coming over later that day, she sought out a homemade *flan* from a *panadería*, a bakery that usually sells to Cubans in pesos. The shop is about five blocks away from their apartment. She also had been going to the *bodega* every day to see if they had any coffee in stock yet; she'd been waiting for 4 days (Cuban coffee is usually a staple in every Cuban household) but none was available. And, she had heard that there was good fish available at the fish shop, so she had waited in line there, too, on this day.

Although Olivia has no children, she is like a grandmother to Elisabeth's grandchildren. She is one of the primary care-givers for Tania, her niece's three-year-old daughter, and, she is also care-giver to Elena, a 13-year-old neighbor girl that she and Elisabeth took in and have raised since Elena was three months old. During our interview, Olivia routinely scolded Tania, brought her food, or encouraged her to go to the bathroom. When I asked Olivia why she didn't have children, she responded:

> I didn't want this . . . I didn't want to get married nor have children. I lived with my (common-law) husband for 8 years and then he left for the U.S. But, I had to take care of my mother who was sick and I could not leave for Miami. Then she died in 1988. But, I couldn't live alone . . . I am diabetic and retired . . . I don't make much money on my pension, so Elisabeth works for both of us. I take care of the house, run errands. I am like the grandmother. Well, usually I take Tania to the *círculo* . . . the one by the transportation center, you know. We love each other a lot . . . I am like her grandmother. (Personal Interview, December, 2001)

Olivia does a lot of the everyday running of the household, even though she is the "dependent" person in the household, the one with the lowest income, no children, and in ill health. Olivia is still an important contributor to the smooth running of the household, to feeding and provisioning for the family, and watching the children. This is an example of how waged or paid labor outside of the home is dependent upon the unpaid labor of someone in the home. The running of the household, indeed, the actual necessity of feeding someone and being able to be there to buy scarce food products, cannot occur unless someone is marginally employed or a full-time worker in the home. Cuban family life survives on this flexibility and unpaid labor. So, Olivia does the shopping, waiting, and negotiating of childcare during the day. In addition, Olivia's sister Elisabeth works as a bathroom attendant at a hotel in Havana and therefore receives tips in dollars. Consequently, she has access to dollars that she shares with her family.

Although creating large households acts as a mechanism of support and casts a wider net, so to speak, of resources for the family, another consequence is the lack of privacy for family members and an increase in family tensions. Part of this has been remedied by sending children to boarding high schools or by trying to build additional rooms in one's home. However, building materials are scarce and it is illegal to build without a permit. Thus, neighborhood groups, such as the Committees in Defense of the Revolution (CDRs) and the Cuban Federation of Women (FMC), try to assist households that are overcrowded by finding scarce resources or offering conflict mediation for families.

Some of the work that Cuban women do in struggling to make ends meet includes skillfully arranging households such that they can increase the number of ration cards to feed the family. Women might bring in an elderly aunt who might receive a higher ration of milk or free up a bedroom to rent. For example, one informant, Bianca, a 50-year-old biologist, married with a grown son, rented her apartment to students while she and her husband lived down the street with her aging parents. Her mother had experienced a slight stroke the year before, but by living with her parents they were able to earn dollars by renting their apartment. This also enabled them to take care of her ailing parents (Personal Interview, December, 2001).

Trans-Continental Family Relations

Cuban families also survive on the monetary support of family members who live permanently outside of Cuba. This includes sending hard currency (dollars) to Cuban relatives on the island and bringing cash and/or other goods into the country for relatives living in Cuba. Only about 20% of the women that I interviewed had family who lived outside of Cuba who sent them money; this is different than those who worked a month or so outside of Cuba and who bring the money home with them. These are family members who live permanently outside of Cuba and send dollars back once a month to family. In the U.S., Cuban Americans can only send $300 every three months to family members in Cuba, a total of $1200 a year. About 30% of Cubans have some outside relation that supports them in this way, a slightly higher percentage than the number of women I interviewed who received help from family members.

The support that many Cubans receive from family outside of Cuba has also created greater stratification in Cuba, both in terms of class and race. For example, most Cubans who left Cuba in the first wave of immigration in the early 1960s were upper class white professionals who settled in the U.S. (Eckstein and Barberia, 2002). Subsequent waves of Cuban immigrants have been more heterogeneous. However, a gap still exists in terms of which Cuban households have family living outside of Cuba. Consequently, the dollars that women receive from family living outside of Cuba allow them certain privileges, such as being able to afford better clothing, more varieties of food, and luxury items such as a television or VCR. This creates stratification between those families who can shop in the dollar economy and those who do not have access to dollars.

One of my informants, Chakita, is a 48-year-old journalist who has a 28-year-old son, David, who lives in New York City. Every three months, David sends Chakita money. He brings along clothing and other goods when he comes to visit. He also has brought a TV, VCR, and stereo, as well as things like shampoo, medicine, and shoes for Chakita and her husband. They live a very comfortable existence with this financial assistance, along with the fact that they are employed in stable jobs working for the state-run newspaper. She is one of the few women I interviewed who lived only with her husband in their household. They own a fairly new three-bedroom apartment. However, this is Chakita's second marriage; when her son was young, she lived with her sister and her mother-in-law helped out as she was going through her divorce. Chakita's living situation is indeed very rare, and were it not for her son, her life would not be quite as comfortable (Personal Interview, October, 2001).

Another respondent, Gabriela, a fifty-year-old woman with two adult children, receives money from her cousin in the U.S. and her son, who lives in Brazil. They both send her money along with other things that she could not afford or that are not available in Cuba, such as Nintendo and a mountain bike. Neighbors used to congregate in her apartment, taking turns playing Nintendo. However, both items she ended up selling when she lost her job in October.

The support from her cousin and her son enabled her to survive the job loss and economic crisis that was de-stabilizing families in the fall of 2001, after the downturn in the Cuban economy. Her family's financial support has also allowed her to help support her grown daughter who lives at home, too.

Gabriela says,

> I've had lots of different jobs, but now it is hard to find a job . . . with the war in Afghanistan and the drop in tourism, to enter or

find new businesses is hard. I have friends here who help . . . my
cousin (in Miami) sends me things, sends money. I can trade on the
underground market or trade things with people to get things. (Personal Interview, December, 2001)

Gabriela's family outside of Cuba is essential in assisting her in making
ends meet, from actually providing cash to sending items that she can
sell on the illegal market for cash.

Family members living outside of Cuba are fundamental to the maintenance not just of individual households, but also to the national economy, which benefits from the increased flow of U.S. dollars in the
country. This allows Cubans to spend dollars in the state-run *tiendas* or
stores. About 30% of the Cuban economy is derived from these family
remittances. More recently, the U.S. has threatened to discontinue allowing Cuban-Americans to send money to family in Cuba. Not only
could this destabilize the Cuban economy, it will have devastating effects on individual Cubans who rely on this support.

The State

The Cuban state provides a number of services and supports for
women who are trying to negotiate multiple demands as parents and
wage earners. For example, women are given one year of paid maternity
leave, with a guarantee that their job will be available upon their return
to work. They are also given subsidized childcare through the state run
círculos.

Many women mentioned the importance of being able to send their
children to school and have them fed during the day. One informant,
Paula, who is a single mother, is able to send her daughter to school and
an afterschool program, known in Cuba as *semi-internado,* for a nominal fee. They also provide a mid-morning and afternoon snack, which
helps Paula, who suffers from depression, with peace of mind about
how her daughter will be fed.

This state-provided support enables women to work and provide financially for their families. Parents pay a nominal fee each month for
child care and mothers are allowed such "luxuries" as cutting to the
head of the line in certain stores in order to get their shopping done more
quickly. Also, doctors, pharmacists, and some other agencies set up special hours for parents, since the state considers mother's time more limited than the average citizen. They are also given subsidized food, and
for families with children under the age of eight, they are guaranteed

items such as milk, eggs, and meat since they have young children who need multiple sources of protein. During one interview, Sonia, a 41-year-old mother of two teenagers said,

> After one year of pregnancy, all the mothers have the rights to obtain a license (paid maternity license) . . . the *círculos* and *semi-internados* help women out as well. This is very important, because the mother begins work, takes her child to school, ends work, and gets the child from school. This is a tremendous alleviation for the mother because all this time the child is taken care of, and it is not just studying, they play and do whatever else, too. (Personal Interview, November, 2001)

The care giving that the state provides allows parents, in most cases, mothers, to engage in economic activity in the formal and informal sector. It also enables mothers to find ways to make ends meet, and most importantly, to secure dollars to feed their families. The *círculos* provide child care from 7 a.m. until 7 p.m., which gives parents the flexibility to work up to 12 hours a day. This allows women time to negotiate transportation to and from work, to find food in out of the way markets, or to make some extra money on the side selling things in the street. The state guarantees women a modicum of support that enables them to combine wage earning and care giving, support that does not occur in many other countries in Latin America or in the U.S.

In addition, the state provides basic food staples for every Cuban family. This includes coffee, sugar, bread, milk, oil, chicken, eggs, and other staples every month. While this is a great help to most Cubans, they also complain about the lack of diversity in food products, the amount of foodstuffs that they receive each month, and the lack of meat and protein goods. For example, one informant, Diana, and her family have difficulties with food shortages. While they are not facing long-term hunger, they do face food insecurities and the family does not have access to dollars. In order to make ends meet they sell things in the street: clothing or toys that they no longer need. One of Diana's daughters, 32-year-old Maria, has a six-year-old daughter, Alma, who is chronically sick, underweight, and is constantly under a doctor's care. Part of her illness can be traced to insufficient protein and food consumption. Although Alma is the only child in their household facing these problems, the family's financial stability and food insecurity has much to do with Alma's illnesses. Their family has no family members living outside of Cuba, and they must make searching for dollars a daily task (Personal Interview, November, 2001).

The state supports them, though, by offering free medical care to all Cubans, which assists with Alma's problems. The state also ensures that there is at least some food for everyone, even if it is not enough or of the greatest variety. Without this help, a family like Diana's would fall into poverty much like families elsewhere in the Third World.

The state also helped to facilitate families' economic survival by introducing dollars into the economy, which helped to stem the growth of the informal economy. This created a means whereby people could work for other companies or work for themselves in order to secure dollars. Thus, the introduction of the dollar economy, the state services for women and children, and free healthcare alleviate the pressure of the economy for Cuban women. It also makes it easier for them to survive global economic changes wrought by both the collapse of the Soviet Union and the changing world economic order.

DISCUSSION: SURVIVING A CRISIS: WHAT IS THE CUBAN DIFFERENCE?

While many others have written about the strategies that low-income families in Latin America and the U.S. have developed in order to make ends meet, there are some important differences in the Cuban case (Lewis, 1975; Visvanathan, Duggan, Nisonoff, and Wiegersma, 1997; Edin and Lein, 1997; Stack, 1974). Certainly, other families in Latin America survive on support from extended family networks or work in the informal economy in order to secure money, either as street vendors or as other workers in the service sector (Ward, 1990; Jelin,1991). However, women in Cuba can rely on several different sources of assistance, particularly from the Cuban state.

First, unlike the trend in much of Latin America where many states are adopting neo-liberal economic policies and privatizing many state services, the Cuban state has not retreated from providing basic necessities for its citizens, such as food, housing, child care, education, and medical care. The Cuban state, while allowing some state-private ventures and allowing individuals to have their own businesses, has intervened to control wages and corporate/individual profits made in the dollar economy. The regulation of the state-private ventures and the dollar economy through a high state tax on earnings made legally in dollars ensures that all Cubans on some level benefit from the increase in hard currency into the economy. For Cubans who work in the tourist industry or who have a license to run a restaurant in their home or who rent a room to foreigners, their dollar earnings are taxed, sometimes at a rate of 50%. This high tax, however, redistributes some of these private earnings.

Second, while many women in developing countries must work in the informal economy to make ends meet they often do this because they are marginalized completely from the formal economy. However, for most women in Cuba, they still work for the state even if they have a dollar business on the side. In addition, the state still provides basic necessities for every family, despite their economic standing. Thus, if a woman's salary goes up, she will not lose her health care or subsidized childcare. This is unlike the sorts of problems that women on welfare in the U.S. face if their earnings increase, which means most likely that they will lose their Medicaid or housing subsidies. The Cuban state, however, provides subsidized housing, food, health, education, and child care for everyone.

Third, as I mentioned earlier, Cuba has also not cut back on its social services, unlike many of its neighboring countries. For example, in the Dominican Republic in the 1980s and 90s, the state withdrew funding for many medical programs in order to pay back debts to the international community (Whiteford in Scheper-Hughes and Sargent, 1998). The loss of funding for public health resulted in an increase in the child and maternal mortality rate. The infant mortality rate doubled between 1978 and 1987 and the maternal mortality rate doubled in the early 1980s. Likewise, Peru's response to its growing debt in the 1980s and 1990s was to privatize many state services. This included passing on the burden of financing health care to individual Peruvians, charging fees for services, many of which poor Peruvians could not afford (Kim, Shakow, Bayona, Rhatigan, and Runim de Celis, in Kim et al., 2000).

In contrast, during Cuba's economic crisis, the state continued to fund healthcare and education, which helped keep the maternal and infant mortality rate stable, a rate that rivals many First World countries. This does not mean that there were not some shortages of food and medicine. The shortages, however, were the result of other economic forces that limited Cuba's access to resources, not the result of a state policy that cut back on the distribution of food and medicine.

In addition, the Cuban state has given a priority to women and children's healthcare and education. While many nations do this, a fundamental difference in the Cuban context is the level of access that Cubans have to health care, childcare, and education. The government in Cuba is very much integrated into the lives of its citizens. Many state services are located on every block or at least within each neighborhood: the family doctors, the child care centers, and the state run food stores.

Government support to households is often delivered through local state-run groups, such as the CDRs, FMC, and the family doctors. These groups help households survive on a daily basis, through helping women find much needed resources to providing a space for weekly meetings where residents share their concerns or needs, thus developing a sense of community among people. One respondent, Rena, said that it was through the CDRs that people got to know their neighbors and help them out with needs, from finding eggs to swapping child care (Personal Interview, May, 2003).

Often government is seen in many countries as a remote, bureaucratic organization that does not know its citizens. In Cuba, the state structure is local, so people can go to their family doctors, teachers, or CDR representatives to get help in finding scarce resources.

Finally, another Cuban difference is the role of *Cubanismo*—the national ethic and identity of shared struggle. Many women spoke of this as essential to helping them survive. For example, after the worst of Hurricane Michelle had passed through Havana, my friend and I sat on our adjoining porches in our dark neighborhood, without water, gas, electricity or light of any kind, with our neighbors Chakita and Hector who discussed this "Cuban-ness" or Cubanismo. They had shared kerosene and water with us during the storm because we had run out of it; they both described the ability with which Cubans adjust to the everyday losses of food, fuel, and water that are common. Chakita said:

> This is the way in Cuba, we are always helping people. We work together. We have to in order to survive. You don't see this in other countries. It is because of our struggle, because we are unique. (Personal Interview, November 2001)

This "different-ness" that Chakita refers to is a Cuban idiosyncrasy to which many of my other informants also referred when I asked them about their relationships of support with neighbors, family members, and community. There is a distinction and "we-ness" that permeates everyday conversation between Cubans about life in Cuba. Cuban national identity is certainly tied to and shaped by struggle, whether it is against the Yankee aggressor, the global economy, the loss of security through natural disaster or even the people's own government.

The local level community organizations, such as the CDRs and family doctors, provide a space for women to access the government right in their own neighborhoods, keeping them close to their communities and in contact with neighbors and government officials, which helps assist them in times of need.

The community groups that meet once a week or month also provide space for women to exchange with one another food, clothing, advice, and other goods, that connects them with one another out of common need. It creates an identity of togetherness that embodies revolutionary ideology and continues the revolutionary struggle. These are the things that make Cuban women's survival strategies markedly different from the experiences of poor women elsewhere.

CONCLUSION

Cuban women make ends meet and feed their families through some of the strategies discussed above: accessing dollars from overseas family members, working in the street, using the state's support or utilizing extensive kin networks. Through these means, Cuban mothers can buy food in dollar stores, pay for their children's school supplies, and buy needed household goods. In addition, multigenerational households enable the sharing of resources among many family members, since usually someone has access to dollars in the home; bartering and exchange between neighbors is important as well. For example, during one interview, as I was speaking to Cecelia, a lower income divorced mother of three, who was unemployed and worked in the streets, her neighbor came in and gave her six eggs in exchange for a ham. Cecelia said that usually she and her neighbors exchanged food, since some families need or like certain items that the other neighbors don't want (Personal Interview, December, 2001).

The state is also important in supporting families' survival. Women use the state to make ends meet, taking advantage of paid maternity leave, after-school programs, and subsidized healthcare.

Despite these difficulties, Cuban mothers are involved in nation-building, through their commitment to making ends meet, through creating family across national boundaries, through creating households with neighbors, and through socializing the next generation. Their communitarian survival efforts have reinforced many of the Revolution's goals of solidarity and equality. The state in turn has not retreated in its support for women and households and continues to hold health and education and children's well-being part of the vanguard of the revolution.

REFERENCES

Benjamin, Media, Collins, Joseph, and Scott, Michael. (1986). *No Free Lunch: Food and Revolution in Cuba Today*. New York: A Food First Book, Grove Press, Inc.

Cervera, Sonia Catasus. (1996). "The Socio-Demographic and Reproductive Characteristics of Cuban Women." in *Latin American Perspectives*. Vol. 23, no. 1, Winter, pgs. 87-98.

DeRose, Laurie, Messer, Ellen, and Millman, Sara. (1998). *Who's Hungry? And, How Do We Know: Food Shortage, Poverty, and Deprivation*. New York: United Nations University Press.

Eckstein, Susan, and Barberia, Lorena. (2002). Grounding Immigrant Generations in History: Cuban Americans and their Transnational Ties. *International Migration Review*. Vol. 36, no. 3, Fall, pgs. 799-837.

Edin, Kathryn, and Lein, Laura. (1997). *Making Ends Meet*. New York: Russell Sage Foundation.

Frank, Michele, and Reed, Gail. (1997). *Denial of Food and Medicine: The Impact of the U.S. Embargo on Health and Nutrition in Cuba*. Washington, D.C.: American Association for World Health, March.

Harriss-White, Barbara, and Hoffenberg, Sir Raymond. (1994). *Food: Multidisciplinary Perspectives*. Cambridge, Massachusetts: Blackwell.

Jelin, Elizabeth. (1991). *Family, Household, and Gender Relations in Latin America*. New York: Routledge, Chapman, and Hall.

Kim, Jim Yong, Millen, Joyce V., Irwin, Alec, and Gersham, John (2000). *Dying for Growth: Global Inequality and the Health of the Poor*. Monroe, Maine: Common Courage Press.

Lewis, Oscar. (1975). *Five Families: Mexican Case Studies in the Culture of Poverty*. New York: Basic Books.

Scheper-Hughes, Nancy, Sargent, Carolyn. (1998). *Small Wars: The Cultural Politics of Childhood*. Berkeley, CA.: University of California Press.

Schwab, Peter. (1999). *Cuba: Confronting the U.S. Embargo*. New York: St. Martin's Griffin.

Smith, Lois, and Padula, Alfred. (1996). *Sex and Revolution: Women in Cuba*. New York: Oxford University Press.

Stack, Carol B. (1974). *All Our Kin*. New York: Harper and Row Publishers.

Suarez, Mayda Alvarez. (1998). "Mujer y Poder en Cuba." In *Temas*. No. 14, Abril/Junio. Pgs. 13-25.

Visvanathan, Nalini, Duggan, Lynn, Nisonoff, Laurie, and Wiegersma, Nan. (1997). *The Women, Gender, and Development Reader*. Atlantic Highlands, N.J.: Zed Books.

Ward, Kathryn. (1990). *Women Workers and Global Restructuring*. Ithaca, N.Y.: ILR Press.

New Rural Poverty:
The Tangled Web of Environmental
Protection and Economic Aid
in Southern Mexico

Nora Haenn

SUMMARY. Scholars, especially those located in Latin America, argue for a new rurality, one that entails changed rural-urban relations and decreasing reliance by rural residents on small-scale farming. Based on an examination of the impacts of three subsidy programs aimed at residents living near Mexico's Calakmul Biosphere Reserve, I suggest these changes reinforce a continued rural poverty. The programs include a series of "conservation-development" initiatives whose architects hoped would decrease the pressure slash-and-burn farmers placed on area forests. In addition, residents of this area participated in agricultural and

Nora Haenn is affiliated with the Department of Anthropology, Box 2402, Arizona State University, Tempe, AZ 85287 (E-mail: nora.haenn@asu.edu).

This research would not have been possible without the aid of the people of Orozco and San Lorenzo. The author hopes that this article serves to voice some of their economic frustrations as well as their ingenuity in dealing with duress. The author offers special thanks to Madelaine Adelman and the editors of *Journal of Poverty* for their encouragement and insightful comments. Richard Wilk's detailed work in household economies and his careful mentoring were both critical for her investigations.

This research was supported by the Wenner Gren Foundation for Anthropological Research and the Fulbright program's U.S.-Mexico Commission for Educational and Cultural Exchange.

[Haworth co-indexing entry note]: "New Rural Poverty: The Tangled Web of Environmental Protection and Economic Aid in Southern Mexico." Haenn, Nora. Co-published simultaneously in *Journal of Poverty* (The Haworth Press, Inc.) Vol. 8, No. 4, 2004, pp. 97-117; and: *Poverty and Inequality in the Latin American-U.S. Borderlands: Implications of U.S. Interventions* (ed: Keith M. Kilty, and Elizabeth A. Segal) The Haworth Press, Inc., 2004, pp. 97-117. Single or multiple copies of this article are available for a fee from The Haworth Document Delivery Service [1-800-HAWORTH, 9:00 a.m. - 5:00 p.m. (EST). E-mail address: docdelivery@haworthpress.com].

97

school subsidies. I compare the relative impact of all these programs on household incomes and consider both the opportunities for social capital these programs represented and their role in the purported "new rurality." *[Article copies available for a fee from The Haworth Document Delivery Service: 1-800-HAWORTH. E-mail address: <docdelivery@haworthpress. com> Website: <http://www.HaworthPress.com> © 2004 by The Haworth Press, Inc. All rights reserved.]*

KEYWORDS. People and parks, PROCAMPO, PRONASOL, environmentalism

Latin American scholars are reexamining poverty in light of a new rurality, *nuevas ruralidades*. This reexamination rests on a shift in rural political and economic structures as well as a shift in thinking. If rural areas were once thought of as backward, agrarian, and boss-dominated regions, today's reality demonstrates that these regions are more than passive players in state economies. Instead, advocates of a new rurality note that, while the primary importance of farming has lessened, Latin America's countryside continues to function as a source of natural resources. At the same time, an increase in national and international migration has deeply entrenched rural peoples' connections to urban centers. These phenomena are the result of acute economic crises in Latin America's countryside, crises precipitated by international policies that favor low-wage labor over subsistence farming and cheap exports over domestic consumption. Despite these crises-driven changes, rural areas continue to present a range of distinctive cultures and economic practices that differ markedly from urban areas. Scholars of the new rurality pay renewed attention to these configurations and the relationship of rural economic structures to poverty (Pérez, 2001).

Here, I discuss the particular role of environmental protection and sustainable development in this new rural setting. Theorists of the new rurality emphasize the way Latin America's countryside "functions as a source of natural resources and primary materials" (Echeverri y Ribero in Pérez, 2001, p. 23), that is, possesses goods that can be converted into manufactured items or tangibles such as clean air and water. In this regard, the move away from a rural economy focused on agriculture and toward one based on migration and wage labor presents a continuous disconnect regarding who benefits from natural resources. Where once rural areas provided food, timber, and other goods to cities, rural sites may now be expected to compensate for the environmental damage caused by industrialization and urban consumption patterns. In the name of environmental protection, rural residents may be expected to sacrifice access to resources critical for their subsistence, such that the new rurality may translate into an old rural poverty.

In order to counter this possibility, environmental protection programs throughout Latin America often include programs aimed at poverty relief. Most recently, these programs have come under fire from environmentalists who believe sustainable development projects distract from the task at hand. Especially in the case of projects that accompany protected areas or national parks, these critics argue that poverty relief has not yet proven to support biodiversity conservation (Oates, 1999; Terborgh, 1999). New critiques from anthropology, in contrast, note that regardless of their effectiveness, many sustainable development programs affect a change in social relations and how people think about the environment (Carrier, m.s.). Whether these changes achieve either goal, of protecting natural resources or improving standards of living for rural peoples, often depends on dynamics specific to each conservation site.

I return to this debate in the paper's conclusions. In the meantime, I offer data that shows, regardless of their impact on wildlife and the environment, many sustainable development programs do little to alleviate poverty. Indeed, in Mexico, the shift in rural economies, combined with a federal imperative to support the rural sector, has long since forced many rural peoples to rely on state handouts for their subsistence. For decades, government programs in Mexico have "pulled and pushed [peasants] out of corn farming" (Cancian, 1992, p. 27). At the same time, the quantity of agricultural programs in the 1970s led some researchers to conclude that Mexican farmers were basically salaried through government credit (see Paré in Hewitt de Alcántara, 1984, p. 154). Caught within a farming system that fails to address their economic concerns and government subsidies that function similarly, many rural Mexicans continue to farm for reasons having to do with their identity, personal dignity, and a lack of alternatives (Haenn, m.s.). Most recently, however, rural poverty is complicated by environmental protection, the state's new tool to manage the economic squeeze of the rural sector.

My data for these assertions come from 14 months of participant-observation in the *municipio* or county of Calakmul, in Mexico's southeastern state of Campeche. Calakmul is an agricultural frontier, colonized by migrant farmers during the past 40 years. During most of that time, residents of the area complained the government paid little attention to them, provided few schools, roads, or health clinics. The region tended to vote for the left-leaning PRD party, an opposition group in a state dominated for most of the 20th century by the PRI party. These electoral and development tensions became more acute when federal authorities decreed the Calakmul Biosphere Reserve in the late 1980s. Internationally, the Reserve served Mexican authorities who touted its million-plus acres of tropical forests. At the time, governments throughout the world were under pressure by international agencies to create park systems (O'Neill, 1996). Locally, these policies were not nearly as popular. In Calakmul, authorities accidentally included numerous villages inside Reserve limits and, at the time, threatened thousands with relocation. Unsurprisingly, the Reserve became a rallying point for local people's social and economic frustrations (Boege, 1995).

Calakmul's *campesinos* (or subsistence farmers) argued forcefully that the Reserve breached a social contract between the state and their community, a contract that combined land and development aid. Outlined in Article 27 of Mexico's constitution, this contract mandated land distribution and agricultural support to Mexico's small-scale farmers. These guarantees were in effect until 1991, when Mexican authorities altered the legal framework of Mexico's agrarian structures. Despite these legal changes, Calakmul's people, like campesinos elsewhere in Mexico (Collier, 1994), used public protests, private grumbling, and the power of their vote to hold the state accountable for these promises.

As I describe in greater detail below, state response to conflicts surrounding the Reserve entailed directing financial support to the region. These monies supported a series of sustainable development projects, whose combined budget, by 1995, likely approached US $1 million per year; monies aimed at just 15,000 people. Authors of the agenda hoped that, collectively, the projects would diversify farm operations in a way that guaranteed greater farm income and appease campesinos (Acopa and Boege, 1998). Through the programs, they envisioned encircling the Reserve, not with a fence, but with supportive campesinos ready to defend the Reserve's existence. Finances were key to motivating this support. A common aphorism in conservation circles states, "If conservation pays, conservation stays."

Consequently, my research questioned the financial impact of these programs. Between 1994 and 1995, I worked with research assistants to document household earnings in the pseudonymous communities of Orozco and San Lorenzo during a period of 6 and 4 months, respectively. On a weekly or bi-weekly basis, we visited with families and reconstructed all monies earned in the intervening time period. I also gathered community level data through interviews with village leaders. At the village level, I questioned how the projects affected social and political dynamics.

Following an overview of the sustainable development programs, I turn to agricultural and education subsidies and compare the three realms both financially and in terms of the kind of state-campesino relations each fostered. This comparison forms the basis of my assertion that sustainable development did relatively little to address poverty concerns in Calakmul. These findings would not be novel to the agenda's architects–including the Reserve Director, managers of a farm organization, and a handful of non-governmental agents. In the mid-1990s, these individuals viewed the programs as experimental. They were unsure whether the series of projects would effectively protect forests or raise people's standard of living.

OVERVIEW: CALAKMUL'S SUSTAINABLE DEVELOPMENT AGENDA

During 1994-95, the villages of Orozco and San Lorenzo were deeply immersed in the sustainable development programs managed by a local farm organization in conjunction with the offices of the Calakmul Biosphere Reserve. The programs reflected Calakmul's population of small-scale farmers living within and close to extensive stands of forest. The Reserve and farm organization offered help in establishing organic agriculture, combining farming with forestry activities, harvesting timber sustainably, managing wildlife, along with environmental education programs. (Hereafter, I refer to this collection of programs as "the sustainable development agenda.") The majority of money supporting these programs came from Mexico's federal government, although a host of international donors also provided funds: the Nature Conservancy, the MacArthur Foundation, the World Bank's Global Environmental Fund, Canada's Eastern Ontario Model Forest, as well as indirect support from the U.S. Agency for International Development.

Each of the sustainable development programs followed a similar outline. Villagers formed a committee which, in turn, requested the project from the farm organization. The organization then sent a university trained staffer (in forestry, agriculture, biology, or veterinary medicine) to the village to explain the project and oversee villagers' implementation. The staffer would estimate sustainable harvests (in the case of timber) and then handle paperwork soliciting a state permit on the villagers' behalf. In the case of products for which there was no local market, the farm organization might distribute saplings, for example for allspice trees, in an effort to create a market for the product.

Closer examination of the wildlife management project shows how the programs worked more specifically. The wildlife management project aimed to show the economic value of hunted species and then follow up with a management plan. Accompanied by the university-trained staffers, and supplied by the project with boots, flashlights and other items, villagers ran nightly transects through their community to document how many and what kinds of animals were on their lands. The most common animals included white-tailed deer, peccary, spider monkeys, and various members of the rodent family. Villagers also volunteered to document animals killed for household consumption. Hunters were supposed to bring their kills to a designated person who noted the species, its sex, weight, and approximate age. At the end of a year, the university-trained staffer presented an estimate of the total kilos of wild meat consumed in a village along with its cash equivalent. With information on animal populations reinforced by data on the cash importance of game meat, villagers had a basis to begin managing their wildlife for long-term hunting. In general, the sustainable development agenda emphasized the monetary value of forest products in the effort to create a forest economy, one that would support forest cover rather than forest clearing.

Despite these similarities across the sustainable development agenda, the programs' impacts on Orozco and San Lorenzo differed because the two communities were distinct in both their natural resources and their overall reliance on government subsidies. Orozco sits on poor quality farming soil, is subject to intense droughts, and families there are able to harvest just one crop per year. San Lorenzo offers better agricultural soils, occupies a more humid location, and families there harvest two crops a year. Orozco lie just half an hour from the headquarters of the Reserve and farm organization spearheading the sustainable development agenda. Travel to San Lorenzo from these same offices took two hours. As a result, Orozcans were more active in (and dependent on) conservation development, while San Lorenzans enjoyed an overall higher standard of living. Overall, the 230 people living in Orozco benefitted from these funds by participating in five of the sustainable development projects. San Lorenzo, a community of 180, participated in four of these projects.

Just how did the sustainable development programs contribute to household income? First, the programs held the possibility of diversifying a family's farm base. Calakmul's people worked mainly in subsistence farming for corn and cash cropping jalapeño chile peppers. While many families added other cultivars to these two crops (including bananas, beans, and rice), corn provided the staple for daily diets and chile peppers were a primary source of cash. Second, campesinos working with the sustainable development programs benefitted from the projects in a number of ways. As an incentive and to compensate people for time spent on the projects (for example, running transects, planting trees, and attending meetings), campesinos might receive an occasional day's wage. The amount was never enough to fully compensate people's time, but could tie a family over when other funds were short. Another popular form of remuneration was the *despensa*, a bag of basic foodstuffs whose costs equaled between one and two days of wage labor. Participants might receive material goods, such as saplings and shovels or, in some cases, boots, flashlights, and bicycles.

In addition to these financial resources, people most active in the sustainable development agenda were able to take advantage of the programs' important social capital. By monopolizing the role of contact person with the program managers, these campesinos became the principal brokers for other governmental and non-governmental groups seeking to implement aid projects in their villages. As arbiters of the projects entering their communities, contact people and brokers–almost always men–benefitted disproportionately from the benefits the sustainable development agenda offered.

It is important to note that Calakmul's sustainable development agenda took place in addition to various other subsidy programs. In the following sections, I review the two most important of these programs, an agricultural subsidy (known as PROCAMPO) and children's scholarships. After a description of each program, I will show how both outweighed the sustainable development agenda in their financial contributions to household income. That is, even though managers of Calakmul's sustainable development agenda worked to be a principal influence in people's financial lives, they had to compete with other state welfare programs. In this competition, the intense social interactions surrounding the sustainable development programs, namely an endless series of meetings, could make the programs appear more financially weighty than they really were. In my experience, Calakmul's people counted more on the agricultural aid in PROCAMPO and the children's scholarships to get them through the year.

AGRICULTURAL SUBSIDIES

Many of the sustainable development projects addressed agricultural issues, however, for Calakmul's farmers, PROCAMPO was the most critical state support for farming. PROCAMPO paid people a fixed sum for each hectare of land (equal to 2.4 acres) planted in pasture or subsistence crops. Because it focused on traditional farming rather than forest products, managers with the Reserve and farm organization did not consider PROCAMPO as fostering sustainable development. Instead, federal authorities created PROCAMPO to compensate small-scale producers for the devaluation in farm goods anticipated with Mexico's entry into the North American Free Trade Agreement. In 1994-95, the program paid 350 pesos per hectare. This amount increased to 440 in 1995-96.

Table 1 outlines the program's specific impact in Orozco and San Lorenzo. As we will see, PROCAMPO contributed more than any other aid program to household incomes. In Table 1, we begin to get a sense of the subsidy's importance by comparing the amount people earned through PROCAMPO to the amount of time it would have taken to earn the same income in the local labor market. This comparison allows me to assess PROCAMPO within the context of Calakmul's regional economy. In dollar amounts, the PROCAMPO payments listed in Table 1 equaled 213 to 290 U.S. dollars. Given local salaries and the cost of living in Calakmul, this amount could have a significant role in people's lives.

Wage labor in Calakmul was calculated by the day. Daily salaries ranged from 15 to 20 pesos. This rate applied to the most widely available work, as farm hand, as well as to government-sponsored jobs programs. The fact that people calculated the wage as a daily rate, as

TABLE 1. Household PROCAMPO Earnings

	Orozco (12 households)	San Lorenzo (33 households)
Avg. # of hectares inscribed in PROCAMPO per household	3.1	4.6
Avg. income from PROCAMPO per household based on 440 pesos/ha	1,496 pesos	2,024 pesos
Equivalent of avg. income in wage labor days (based on 20 pesos/day)	75 days	101 days

opposed to an hourly or weekly rate, indicates the uneven quality of job availability. Not unusually, men worked two or three days a week in wage labor and spent the rest of their time in their own fields. Women had very few job opportunities and tended to work in wage labor only during the harvest season, when jobs become plentiful. A few government employees in Calakmul could count on regular salaries. For the majority of Calakmul's people, however, cash income was sporadic at best.

In making the comparison between PROCAMPO and wage labor in Table 1, I chose the 20 peso rate. This amount conveys a best case scenario and addresses the way wage labor during my research was undergoing upward pressure to the 20 peso mark. At this exchange, PROCAMPO payments in the village of Orozco offered the equivalent of two and a half months of work. In San Lorenzo, where the community's two annual harvests allowed people to inscribe more hectares in the program, the subsidy equaled more than three months of wage labor work.

PROCAMPO payments were so large, they often outpaced what families earned in the area's principal cash crops, jalapeño chile peppers and *chihua*, a kind of squash harvested for pumpkin seeds. Furthermore, PROCAMPO had few of the drawbacks of cash cropping. Payments arrived even if harvests failed. Cash crops often required farmers to enter into exploitative relations with buyers. These men might advance farmers cash, fertilizers, or other goods in exchange for exclusive access to an individual's crop at harvest time. This point, along with collusion among chile buyers, effectively depressed chile prices. PROCAMPO carried none of these complications. Instead, PROCAMPO stood as a relatively trustworthy source of income, although the timing of these disbursements followed no set schedule, and campesinos were never sure just when the monies would arrive.

In 1994-95, the bulk of state aid entering Calakmul households centered on farming. By 2001, this emphasis would shift dramatically as state agents supported children's education and women's healthcare to a much greater degree (Haenn & Atencio, m.s.). The children's scholarships of the mid-1990s presaged this change while offering, for many families, the second largest source of state aid to their household income. Children's scholarships are also important to my analysis because they provide an opportunity to highlight the social engineering linked to many subsidies in Calakmul. Scholarships included a decision-making framework that, while at first glance appears empowering, ultimately bespeaks a government arbitrated empowerment. As I ex-

plain it below, this framework, repeated at the regional farm organization and in other development settings, saw its original radicalism strain
under the weight of repetition and top-down development planning.

IN SOLIDARITY WITH STATE AID

Children's scholarships aimed to support first, second, and third-grad-
ers at risk of dropping out of school because of their parents' poverty. In
addition to cash payments of 118 pesos monthly, children received a
despensa, or bag of basic foodstuffs worth about 25 pesos. Effective even
during vacation months, the scholarships plus despensas annually
equaled 86 days of wage labor. People depended on what were supposed
to be monthly scholarships for a steady stream of income. During my research, however, payments arrived at irregular and unpredictable inter-
vals.

Children's scholarships were part of a multi-faceted, nation-wide program known as PRONASOL, the National Solidarity Program or, more
simply, Solidarity. Solidarity linked the scholarships to a number of other
aid programs and a specific governing structure which ostensibly empowered Mexico's poor. Solidarity funds also supported the sustainable
development agenda, water catchment tanks, school buildings, and rural
stores. Ideally, Solidarity paid for proposals that arose from campesino
self-reflection, where campesinos evaluated their situation and requested
help with what they saw as their more urgent needs. Solidarity officials
asserted that their funding would not constitute a handout. Instead, projects would come to fruition only if campesinos contributed labor or
funds. In this way, Solidarity structures resonated with notions of participatory planning processes prevalent in international development circles
(Chambers, 1994). Throughout Mexico, Solidarity committees, such as
Calakmul's farm organization, were set up to coordinate development activities. Programs such as the children scholarships required additional
subcommittees at the village level. (For an assessment of the scholarship
program nationally, see Gershberg, 1994.) Because government agents
tried to channel empowerment toward government aims, Calakmul's
people were doubtful of these efforts.

In the case of children's scholarships, the prescribed program of
self-reflection underwent some alteration, even though, as with Solidarity programs more generally, the scholarships asked recipients to identify themselves and their neighbors as poor. A Solidarity pamphlet
shared with me by parents in San Lorenzo proposed the grade schoolers,

not parents or teachers, choose scholarship recipients. The authors suggested designating "A Special Day" when children would "freely and spontaneously" elect scholarship winners. Through games and other activities, the children would consider who among them had the most financial need and the most academic interest (not academic achievement). Adults guiding the children should only assure that elected children indeed presented financial need and that no single family received more than one scholarship.

Orozcans and San Lorenzans disregarded these guidelines, such that I never heard mention of them. The San Lorenzan who shared the pamphlet did so as a gesture of good will and gave no indication he had read the material. Instead, the communities' parent-teacher associations chose scholarship recipients. Most families with a school-age child received a scholarship. Rather than focus on first- and second-graders, scholarships followed a single child throughout his or her grade-school years. Upon the child's graduation, parents and teachers assured a family's continued participation by passing the scholarship onto a younger sibling. The notion that scholarships support school attendance was watered down as the money became a critical component of a family's overall subsidy profile.

Because numerous programs in Calakmul mimicked Solidarity's participatory decision-making processes, the potential radicalism such processes might hold were weakened in Calakmul. Solidarity structures drew on penetrating critiques of government practices in Latin America dating back to the 1960s. At that time, liberation theologians and other social activists sponsored campaigns of self-reflection as a tool of consciousness raising among impoverished people. Peasants explored how their poverty was the result of government disregard and economic structures that prohibited their advancement (Boff, 1988). Campesinos then discussed solutions to these obstacles and, in subsequent decades, pressed for altered political and economic structures (Alvarez et al., 1998). In their appropriation of liberation theology and infusion of development aid, Solidarity organizers at Calakmul aimed at preventing the kind of militancy that resulted when peasants throughout Latin America, having their peaceful proposals meet government oppression and violence, turned to armed struggle (Harvey, 1998). Indeed, Calakmul's Reserve Director and farm organization managers explicitly connected their efforts to Mexico's Zapatista uprising of 1994. The Zapatistas surprised Mexicans and the world by presenting organized, militant demands for social, economic, and cultural equality. Although Calakmul's conservation-development agenda began years before the uprising, in the event's retelling, Calakmul authorities argued that aid, in part, was meant to quell the kind of rebelliousness found in the Zapatista movement.

These complicated social aims merit further discussion than I am able to give here (but see Haenn, m.s.). For example, scholars argue another aim of Solidarity entailed tying the programs to their figurehead, Mexico's former president Salinas de Gortari. (For an overview of Solidarity, see Cornelius et al., 1994. For the program's origination in the World Bank's re-evaluation of its treatment of the poor, see Díaz-Polanco, 1997.) Salinas made conspicuous visits to inaugurate Solidarity projects and reinforce not only the state's role as a welfare agent, but also the connection between his political party and financial patronage. These points should alert readers to the complex motivations inherent in the financial accountings noted below.

SUBSIDY IMPACTS ON HOUSEHOLD INCOME

Calakmul's diverse poverty relief programs carried different opportunities and constraints in people's wider economic and social worlds. All in all, the conservation-development programs carried constraints of time, energy, and, ultimately, money as people shifted away from more assuredly lucrative work of cash cropping and subsistence farming. Coincidentally, conservation-development carried the most social opportunities as the programs linked campesinos to one another and state agents in a series of meetings and collective efforts. As noted earlier, economic and social gain could achieve a certain coevalness when people were able to transform their personal networks into access to additional aid programs. But, not all state programs offered either significant economic or social gain.

Even spurious aid could add to the sense that Calakmul's people were supported by a web of state aid. Hardly a week passed in Orozco or San Lorenzo without a visit by a governmental or non-governmental agent to address village members' health, economic development, or land management. One day, I was surprised by a state healthcare team who barged unannounced into my house to vaccinate any children present. Employees of the state Integral Family Development program gave Orozco's women a surprise Mother's Day gift when they delivered bags of food, t-shirts, and water bottles. The agents deposited a pile of goods on the village's square, took publicity photos of the bewildered recipients, and quickly departed.

Table 2 examines the relative contribution of diverse income sources for six Orozcan and four San Lorenzan households. The information for Orozco covers a 6-month period from January through June 1995. The information for San Lorenzo covers a 3-month period from August through October 1995. Because of the different time periods involved, data collection in Orozco missed PROCAMPO distribution as well as the chihua squash harvest. Data collection in San Lorenzo missed the chile harvest.

The chart requires additional explanation. The final column tallies the household's total peso amount of earnings. The column "miscellaneous sales" includes products other than chile or chihua, such as corn, beans, chickens, eggs, as well as sales from a family-run store. Under the title, "conservation, development," I have separated out household income stemming from state programs that had some ecological goal. For San Lorenzo, *none* of these wages and despensas were derived from the Reserve and farm organization sources noted above. For Orozco, *all* such wages stemmed from the Reserve and farm organization, while roughly half the despensas arrived from the same source.

Table 2, thus, demonstrates conservation-development's relative importance during periods when state subsidies were less available to farmers. As such, the figures are provocative both for what they relate and what they fail to relate. Families like that of Jerónimo and Venancio, which controlled development projects as they entered the community, actually received a relatively small proportion of their income from state sources. These families tended to be among the better off, and development programs comprised one of several strategies they used to make ends meet. Jerónimo exemplified this group. Jerónimo stood out as the wealthiest villager in Orozco. As the only household to own a refrigerator and television, the family sold sodas, ice, and popsicles to fellow villagers who gathered each evening to watch soap operas. State sponsored projects contributed only 16% to his overall income.

The table also shows how the development setting in Orozco differed from that of San Lorenzo. Extremes in Orozcans' dependence on aid reflected the community's overall lack of resources as well as an internal hierarchy that cut some people off from state aid. Romero's family was part of a class of people denied access to development aid because they were relatively new to the community. Long-term residents of Orozco required new neighbors wait a number of years before allowing them access to aid. Established families like Orozco's Eusebio's participated very little in development programs, but their overall income was so

TABLE 2. Sources of Income as % Contribution to Overall Income

	Cash Crops	Misc. Sales	Wage Labor	Cons, Dev'p Wages & Despensas	Children's Scholarships	PRO-CAMPO	% Inc. Subsidies	Total Inc. in pesos
Orozco								
Jerónimo	61%	23%	0%	6%	10%	0%	16%	5,941
Gerardo	59%	6%	9%	5%	20%	0%	25%	2,903
Venancio	25%	15%	0%	51%	9%	0%	60%	6,795
Paco	47%	12%	22%	19%	0%	0%	19%	1,350
Eusebio	0%	0%	50%	12%	38%	0%	50%	1,562
Romero	5%	2%	92%	1%	0%	0%	1%	4,084
San Lorenzo								
Ramón	69%	0%	4%	9%	18%	0%	28%	3,312
Alejandro	5%	0%	0%	45%	19%	32%	96%	5,584
Melitón	0%	0%	28%	27%	0%	45%	72%	1,935
Carlos	10%	10%	22%	8%	6%	44%	58%	4,039

low that even sporadic inputs could form a significant source of earnings. In San Lorenzo, Alejandro stood out from his neighbors as he combined farming with work as village health promoter. This position proved most beneficial. During the study period he and a son participated in a well-paid, state-sponsored workshop that caused the percentage of household income from development aid to balloon to 95%.

The overall importance of these subsidies in the early 1990s is greater still in light of the scarce employment then available in the Calakmul region. Only a few full-time jobs were available in the county's commercial center or with the various development projects. Large-scale chile producers hired seasonal laborers during the harvest. At these times, villages became nearly empty as all able bodied adults and children took advantage of the opportunity. Some family members traveled to neighboring cities or to Mexico's Caribbean coast where more jobs were available. However, unlike in other parts of Mexico, this kind of migration had not yet become a permanent part of a household's earning strategies. This situation would change in the late 1990s, when migration to the U.S. became a prominent feature of Calakmul's economy. In the meantime, in 1995, families like that of Eusebio's in Orozco lived on little more than US $1/day, while the wealthiest families in the sample earned US $8/day. As noted earlier, figures in the final column of Table 2 are noted in pesos. At 20 pesos a day for wage labor, each 1,000 in earnings depicted in Table 2 was the equivalent of 50 days of work. During their respective time periods, Orozcans earned between 67 and 300 days in wage labor equivalency (again, for the 6-month period) and San Lorenzans earned between 50 and 275 days in wage labor equivalency (for the 3-month period).

A second glance at Table 2 shows corn's absence from considerations of household income. The reasons for this arose partly from the fact that the value of corn in Mexico has dropped to such an extent, that few of Calakmul's people viewed it as a source of cash. In this regard, the situation at Calakmul was similar to that of subsistence producers throughout Mexico (de Janvry et al., 1994). The crop that was critical to campesino survival held little remunerative worth in the marketplace. Social activists decline to mention corn's exact market value because they believe the low price inadequately portrays the importance of corn to subsistence farmers. These activists assert the ability to feed oneself and one's family is priceless. In pushing families out of farming, state policies force people into Mexico's erratic wage labor market, one which offers no substitute for food security (Collier, 1994). By avoiding mention of corn's market value, activists hope to soften, in whatever small way, these pressures on campesino families.

Sustainable development projects can similarly insert people into wage labor markets and may help foster a rural poverty devoid of subsistence production. Interestingly, not a few of Calakmul's people might be glad to take this route, backbreaking as farming is. In order to do so, however, these campesinos explicitly or implicitly rely on other state aid programs. Campesinos agreed, however, this reliance was risky. Both the amount and timing of state aid was unreliable, and this unreliability had specific consequences for campesino livelihoods.

UNRELIABLE AID

Calakmul's farmers would likely disagree with my depiction of them as beneficiaries of government aid. The prominence of government cash handouts was offset by a few factors. Payments rarely arrived as scheduled. Families passed months without seeing money owed to them, only to receive a sudden windfall. Once the money did arrive, managing it presented a problem. There were no banks in the Calakmul region. Local merchants capitalized their businesses by taking in people's savings and paying interest, but this system was not always trustworthy. Campesinos had no recourse when shop owners chose to abscond with the funds. For all these reasons, budgeting so brief bonanzas might carry a family throughout the year could prove most challenging. The unreliability of government aid gave people cause to argue they were not themselves dependent on such income.

The second point that detracted from the cash handouts was their use as a substitute for infrastructure building and regional planning. For example, in late 1995, two hurricanes buffeted Calakmul, destroying the year's crops for most families. (Government agents immediately implemented a program to replace lost corn harvests.) San Lorenzo, where I was living at the time, lay at the end of a thirty-kilometer road so rife with pot holes that traveling the road took an hour. After the hurricanes, floods undermined the road's foundation to such an extent that springs gurgled up from the center of the potholes. This road provided more than 1,000 people their only access to markets and jobs. Soon after the rains, authorities issued an early disbursement of PROCAMPO payments. Flushed with cash, farmers overlooked government negligence in road repair. The road remained impassable into the new millennium.

Unsurprisingly, because of the unreliability in both the subsidies and the broader economic infrastructure, most of Calakmul's people struggled between short-term and long-term usages of aid. This point especially affected the sustainable development programs. Agroforestry, wildlife management and sustainable timber harvests were all long-term programs whose future financial benefit was unknown. Should farmers risk investing time and energy in these projects, or were they better off cultivating short-term aid? The answer to this question was often personal. Individuals more active in the welfare game cultivated as many aid programs as they could manage.

As hinted at above, a changing rural economy entails changes in both private sector opportunities and the quality and content of state aid. In the next section, I discuss how an environment framed by sustainable development lies captive to this flux. At the same time, I concur with commentaries (Brechin et al., 2002) in noting that eliminating sustainable development from the conservationists' tool kit would be problematic. Instead, as rural economies transform, sustainable development programs need to meet people's changing relationship to their physical surroundings.

ENVIRONMENTAL PROTECTION AND ECONOMIC AID IN THE NEW RURALITY

The conditions of the new rurality help to disentangle the web of environmental protection and economic aid in Calakmul by requiring researchers and development practitioners to revisit both the economic setting in rural areas and the quality of rural-urban connections. Here, sustainable development can open some avenues of poverty relief while closing or reconfiguring other avenues. That such openings and closings are deeply cultural is the mark of any conservation setting. As Carrier (m.s.) notes, what people mean by environment differs across distinct settings, and, more critically, people change their environmental definitions as they move among diverse social groups. Sustainable development has been a useful concept because it helps translate these diverse meanings into more commonly shared notions. At least one author has called sustainable development a "meta-fix" (Dobson, 1998), an all-purpose patch that smooths over social and cultural differences. In making this leap, however, conservationists and local people may commodify the physical environment in ways uncomfortable to both groups. By translating the value of an environment into a peso or dollar figure, conservation becomes a game of catch-up. For example, how can the price of forested carbon sink (in which forests reputedly offset pollution emitted by factories) compare to the value of that same forest in timber? A commodified environment may mean the devaluing of certain, crucial ecological components. The question of corn and a family's ability to feed itself serves as an example here.

In Calakmul's insecure economic setting, people appeared willing to engage in untried sustainable development programs for combined political and financial reasons–to gain increased services from state authorities, and to cultivate a more congenial relationship with the ruling PRI party. But, comparing the aims of PROCAMPO and the children's scholarships, we see how, as a package deal, the programs required campesinos to confront contradictory messages which placed their livelihoods at stake. Ostensibly, both programs supported the family farm as it existed. In reality, the programs pulled family farms in two different directions.

PROCAMPO reinforced long standing farming norms. PROCAMPO supported subsistence crops, such as corn, beans, and rice. The program, thus, suggested farmers' time was better spent on these endeavors rather than untried, new sustainable farm methods. Children's scholarships, however, negated the value of farming altogether. By the turn of the 21st century, children's scholarships extended to *secundaria*, the secondary school years roughly equivalent to U.S. middle school. Calakmul's residents widely believe this added schooling meant their children would no longer be interested in farming. The notion of an educated campesino was a contradiction in local cultural terms. Where PROCAMPO reinforced adults' roles in a limited form of farming, children's scholarships encouraged a new generation to get out of farming altogether.

This is not to say that neither PROCAMPO nor the scholarships lacked individual merit. PROCAMPO payments were crucial to many families' survival. Recall Eusebio's family that lived on just US $1/day. Also, children's scholarships held the potential for improving quality of life in ways other than financial. This was especially the case for girls who generally were at a disadvantage in Calakmul's male-dominated society. What I want to emphasize here is that these programs sent mixed messages regarding how the state valued campesinos' principal occupation. As a whole, the programs suggest the new rurality in Calakmul would entail less farming, but what other occupations might be forthcoming was left unclear. In a changing economic base, the mixed messages offered by aid programs reinforced the notion of an insecure economic future and continued short-term thinking. Both of these points worked against the sustainable development agenda, which required a long-term framework.

Campesino insecurity and doubts regarding the future sit awkwardly with Mexico's claims to care for its citizenry, a caring that often translated into paternalism. Paternalism was evident in the directions for selecting scholarship recipients. In agricultural programs, we saw paternalism in the way these subsidies suggested the state knew what was best for farmers to plant. This paternalism further relates to construction of rural-urban connections in Calakmul. PROCAMPO and children's scholarships act as rural-urban connections. Both programs were designed by urban elites and administered locally by university-trained technical staff. Conservation-development had a similar structure. Although conservation-development is relatively new to rural Latin America, its location within this paternalist conduit can make the programs feel, for campesinos, quite similar to past state aid.

Given these points, whether the new rurality is really new is somewhat open to debate, at least in the case of Calakmul. Rural-urban connections for Calakmul include a series of demands that put the squeeze on farming operations and increase people's economic vulnerability. By 2001, a few local environmentalists questioned why, given their dependence on state aid, campesinos farmed at all. They doubted the need for flexibility when it came to the slash-and-burn farming techniques used throughout Calakmul. This point overlooked the dignity campesinos find in subsistence work, the difficulty in assessing a value to corn farming, as well as the complications of state aid noted above. As we saw earlier, in many ways, this phenomenon is long-standing in rural Mexico. Pushing and pulling people out of corn farming is a task that has stretched across the generations.

What is new is the way environmentalism and sustainable development have become added tools in this process. In part, the reason for this is that the "sustainable" aspect of sustainable development remains open to doubt. Without a clear understanding of how this kind of development is novel, sustainable programs tend to operate along the lines of past development aid. Additionally, in the new rurality or the old, state authorities and urbanites demand campesinos provide certain services, behave in certain ways, and maintain certain class positions, all of which effectively deny rural residents political and economic strength.

WORKS CITED

Acopa, D.& E. Boege. (1998). The Maya Forest in Campeche, Mexico: Experiences in Forest Management at Calakmul. In R. Primack, D. Bray, H. Galletti, and I. Ponciano (Eds.). *Timber, Tourists, and Temples: Conservation and Development in the Maya Forest of Belize, Guatemala, and Mexico.* (Pp. 81-97). Washington, D.C.:Island Press.

Boege, E. (1995). *The Calakmul Biosphere Reserve Mexico.* Paris: South-South Cooperation Program, U.N.E.S.C.O.

Boff, L. (1988). *When Theology Listens to the Poor.* San Francisco: Harper & Row.

Brechin, S., P. Wilshusen, C. Fortwanger,& P. West (2002). Beyond the Square Wheel: Toward a More Comprehensive Understanding of Biodiversity Conservation as Social and Political Process. *Society and Natural Resources, 15,* 41-64.

Cancian, F. (1992). *The Decline of Community in Zinacantan: Economics, Public Life, and Social Stratification 1960-1987.* Stanford: Stanford University Press.

Carrier, J., Ed. (m.s.) *Confronting Environments: Local Environmental Understanding in a Globalising World*

Chambers, R. (1994). The Origins and Practice of Participatory Rural Appraisal. *World Development 22,* 953-969.

Collier, G. (1994). *Basta! Land and the Zapatista Rebellion in Chiapas.* Oakland, CA, Food First.

Cornelius, W., A. Craig, & J. Fox, Eds. (1994). *Transforming State-Society Relations in Mexico: The National Solidarity Strategy.* La Jolla, California, Center for U.S.-Mexican Studies, University of San Diego.

de Janvry, A.., E. Sadoulet, & G. Gordillo de Anda (1994). *NAFTA and Mexico's Corn Producers.* Berkeley: University of California, Berkeley, Department of Agricultural and Resource Economics.

Díaz-Polanco, H. (1997). *La rebelión Zapatista y la autonomía.* México, D.F., Mexico: Siglo XXI Editores.

Dobson, A. (1998). *Justice and the Environment: Conceptions of Environmental Sustainability and Theories of Distributive Justice.* Oxford, U.K.: Oxford University Press.

Gershberg, A. I. (1994). Distributing Resources in the Education Sector: Solidarity's Escuela Digna Program.. In W. Cornelius, A Craig, and J Fox (Eds.), *Transforming State-Society Relations in Mexico: The National Solidarity Strategy* (Pp. 233-253). San Diego, California: Center for U.S.-Mexican Studies, University of San Diego.

Haenn, N. (2000). *Biodiversity is Diversity in Use: Community-Based Conservation in the Calakmul Biosphere Reserve.* Arlington, Virginia: The Nature Conservancy. (m.s., 2005, expected). *Fields of Power, Forests of Discontent: Culture, Conservation, and the State in Southern Mexico.* Tucson: University of Arizona Press.

Haenn, N. & C. Atencio. (m.s.). "Progress in *Progresa*?: A Regional Examination of Mexican Health and Education Benefits."

Harvey, N. (1998). *The Chiapas Rebellion: The Struggle for Land and Democracy.* Durham, NC: Duke University Press.

Hewitt de Alcántara, C. (1984). *Anthropological Perspectives on Rural Mexico.* London: Routledge & Kegan Paul.

Oates, J. (1999). *Myth and Reality in the Rain Forest: How Conservation Strategies Are Failing in West Africa*. Berkeley: University of California Press.

O'Neill, K. (1996) The International Politics of National Parks. *Human Ecology 24*, 521-539.

Pérez, C. E. (2001). Hacia una nueva visión de lo rural. In N. Giarracca (Ed.), *Una nueva ruralidad en América Latina?* (Pp. 17-29). Buenos Aires: Consejo Latinoamericano de Ciencias Sociales.

Terborgh, J. (1999). *Requiem for Nature*. Washington, D.C.: Island Press.

THOUGHTS ON POVERTY
AND INEQUALITY

Operation Pedro Pan:
One Family's Journey to the U.S.

Maria Vidal de Haymes

I am an immigrant and in many ways the migration story of my family is similar to that of any other immigrant family in this nation. My family came to the United States in the 1960s, like many before them, lured by the promise of political liberties and economic opportunities. In exchange, we left behind our country, community, friends, and family members. Not unlike other immigrants, my parents' initiation to their new home was marked by insecurity, financial struggle, discrimination, indignities in the work place, and attempts to learn English and understand a new culture.

However universal these immigrant experiences may be, migration accounts may also be viewed from another perspective, one that places the particularity of individual experience in the broader context of the

Maria Vidal de Haymes is affiliated with Loyola University Chicago, School of Social Work, 820 N. Michigan Ave., Chicago, IL 60611.

[Haworth co-indexing entry note]: "Operation Pedro Pan: One Family's Journey to the U.S." Vidal de Haymes, Maria. Co-published simultaneously in *Journal of Poverty* (The Haworth Press, Inc.) Vol. 8, No. 4, 2004, pp. 119-123; and: *Poverty and Inequality in the Latin American-U.S. Borderlands: Implications of U.S. Interventions* (ed: Keith M. Kilty, and Elizabeth A. Segal) The Haworth Press, Inc., 2004, pp. 119-123. Single or multiple copies of this article are available for a fee from The Haworth Document Delivery Service [1-800-HAWORTH, 9:00 a.m. - 5:00 p.m. (EST). E-mail address: docdelivery@haworthpress.com].

http://www.haworthpress.com/web/JPOV
Digital Object Identifier: 10.1300/J134v08n04_07

relationship between the sending and receiving states. It is from this vantage point that I will tell my family migration and resettlement story, which was deeply influenced by the nature of Cuban and U.S. relations.

January 1, 1959, marked the overthrow of Fulgencio Batista by the Movimiento 26 de Julio, the revolutionary organization led by Fidel Castro. In the first months and years of the new revolutionary government sweeping changes were made, including: bringing to trial the former Batista regime officials, the passage of the Agrarian Reform Law that expropriated over 1000 acres of farmland and forbade foreign land ownership; the nationalization of U.S. and foreign owned property; the resumption of diplomatic relations between Cuba and the Soviet Union; and the declaration of Castro that he is "a Marxist-Leninist, and will be one until the last day of [his] life." The U.S. responded with similarly dramatic actions which included: the imposition of an economic embargo on Cuba; a break in diplomatic relations with Cuba; execution of a U.S. supported Cuban exile invasion in Cuba at the Bay of Pigs; and the initiation of Operation Mongoose, a plan of covert actions targeting Cuban leaders and infrastructure.

It was in this context that my family decided to make the ninety mile trip from the shores of Cuba to the U.S. We came in parts, with my brothers being the first to come. The decision to send them ahead was made by my parents amid the rumors of a coming "patria postetad," a document that allegedly would order all children over the age of three into State care for the purposes of indoctrinating them with "Castroism." Fear of losing their children to the state made exiling their children an attractive option for many Cuban parents, including mine who sent my brothers to the U.S. through the Pedro Pan (Peter Pan) program.

Operation Pedro Pan was a clandestine State Department-backed program that smuggled visas into Cuba and children out of Cuba. Over 14,000 Cuban children were secretly brought into the United States between December 26, 1960 and October 21, 1962 under this program that ultimately involved the CIA, the Catholic church, and multiple civic groups in an effort to find caretakers for the Cuban children arriving through the program. Scholars who have recently begun to investigate and document the Pedro Pan Operation have noted that it was the largest organized political exodus of children in this hemisphere, yet the U.S. government kept the program so secretive that some of the participants in the program are just now finding out that they were among the Pedro Pan children (Conde 1999). As knowledge of the Operation has grown, so has controversy regarding its nature and purpose. Castro detractors have charged that, at best, these youth were used as political pawns in a cold war conflict, and, at worst, they were exploited in a CIA plot to disrupt and destabilize the new Cuban government by dislocating families and depriving the Castro government of the contributions of promising youth. Supporters of Castro have positioned Pedro Pan as a grand humanitarian operation, in the tradition of the World War II European kindertransport that saved Jewish children from the reach of the Nazis (Torres 2003).

Controversy withstanding, my brothers, who were 12 and 15 years old at the time, came to the U.S. in 1961. When they arrived at Miami International Airport, they were received by representatives of Monsignor Bryan O. Walsh, Director of the Catholic Welfare Services for the Archdiocese of Miami, who was charged with the care and resettlement of children coming through Operation Pedro Pan. After a brief stay in Miami for processing, my brothers were sent to Lincoln, Nebraska to live in Cristo Rey, a former Catholic orphanage that was reopened to serve as a residential facility for the unaccompanied Cuban youth. They lived there with about 50 other Cuban boys and girls awaiting the arrival of their parents. Initially, like many other Cuban parents, mine expected that they would be separated from their children only a few months while they obtained visas to travel to the United States or until the Cuban government changed, as many Cubans expected at that time. However, the events of the October 1962 Cuban missile crisis created a serious rupture. Commercial flights between Cuba and Miami abruptly ended leaving children in the U.S., while their parents were stranded on the island, unable to join them. What was to have been a brief separation for the 14,000 youth turned into a protracted or permanent separation for many. Numerous children, now scattered over 35 states, remained in foster homes and orphanages under the care of the Catholic Church for many years. Some were never reunited with their parents, while many others did not see their parents again until they were adults with families of their own.

The Cuban Missile Crisis began on October 14th when a U.S. reconnaissance aircraft photographed Soviet construction of intermediate-range missile sites. Numerous responses were considered by the Kennedy administration, ranging from an armed invasion of Cuba to air strikes against the missiles. In the end, Kennedy issued a demand that Premier Khrushchev remove all the missile bases and their nuclear contents, while Kennedy ordered a naval blockade of Cuba to prevent Russian ships from bringing additional missiles and construction materials to the island. In response, Khrushchev authorized the Soviet field commanders stationed in Cuba to launch tactical nuclear weapons in the event of a U.S. invasion. For seven days, the two greatest nuclear super-powers remained deadlocked, teetering on the brink of nuclear war, until on October 28, Khrushchev conceded to Kennedy's demands by agreeing to remove the missiles from Cuba and ordering all Soviet supply ships away from Cuban waters. It was on this same day that I was born in Cienfuegos, Cuba. My mother had traveled to Cienfuegos the last week of her pregnancy because the physicians in Trinidad, our hometown, had been strategically relocated, along with others across the island, in preparation for war. Meanwhile, my brothers remained in Nebraska awaiting reunification.

Unlike most of the other Pedro Pan children, my brothers were fortunate in that they did not have to wait much longer. On the evening of July 2, 1963, my parents, my great aunt, my sister and I departed from Havana on the S. S. Maximus and disembarked from the ship at the Everglades Port the following morning. Our trip had been sponsored by the U.S. Red Cross, as part of a medical supply exchange program. The ship had unloaded its cargo of donated pharmaceuticals and medical supplies and returned to the U.S. with its new cargo of Cuban passengers. This trip was not typical. We had come to the U.S. during a time when relatively few Cubans were able to. Only 50,000 Cubans entered the United States between October of 1962 following the suspension of commercial flights, and before the initiation of the Freedom Flights in November of 1965, which resumed flights between Cuba and the United States, bringing about 250,000 Cubans into the U.S. between 1966 and 1973.

Like my brothers before us, upon our arrival, we spent a short time in Miami for processing before continuing on to Nebraska to join them. We were greeted at the airport by my brothers and Father Tuchek, the Director of Cristo Rey and of Catholic Charities in Lincoln, Nebraska. We were settled into a three-bedroom house that had been rented and filled with donated second-hand furniture in preparation for the arrival of my family. In the ensuing months we continued to receive many resources to support us in our transition to the United States. Most of these resources were funded through the Cuban Refugee Resettlement Program. Unlike many other immigrant groups, Cubans were considered to be political immigrants, afforded refugee status by the U.S. government during the Cold War era. With this status designation came a firm helping hand via the Refugee Program. This program offered a wide array of services and benefits including employment opportunities, financial assistance, health services, surplus food distribution, training and education subsidies, funds for resettlement, assistance to local public schools for bilingual programs, retraining programs for professionals, college tuition loans, and reimbursement to voluntary relief agencies providing daily necessities of refugees.

More than forty years have passed since my family migrated to the U.S. Since then we all became U.S. citizens and my siblings and I have completed school, formed families, had children born here and buried our parents in the United States. During this time the U.S. has had ten different presidents and the Soviet Union collapsed in 1991, ending the annual $4 billion subsidy to Cuba. However, two things have remained unchanged: Fidel Castro has continued in power and U.S. policy toward Cuba persists to be defined by the embargo, despite periodic initiatives toward improving relations between the two countries. Rooted in a Cold War era that ended years ago, the embargo has failed to achieve U.S. policy goals and has damaged U.S. economic, diplomatic and national security interests. It has also severely restricted travel to Cuba, keeping the U.S./Cuba relations barrier in force between family members on either side of the Florida Straights. If the embargo policy ever made sense, it certainly does not now. A lot has changed in forty years and it is time to change the embargo policy.

REFERENCES

Conde, Yvonne M. (1999) *Operation Pedro Pan: The Untold Exodus of 14,048 Cuban Children*. New York: Routledge.
Torres, Maria de los Angeles. (2003). *The Lost Apple: Operation Pedro Pan, Cuban Children in the U.S., and the Promise of a Better Future*. Boston: Beacon Press.

Poverty, Crisis and Resilience of Spirit

Mauricio Cifuentes

Concepcion is seated in front of me as she has been once a week for the last twelve weeks for her therapy session. Throughout this time, she has told me a story of abuse and neglect, her own story. She has put together pieces of information with no evidence of strong emotions. But today, there is something different.

It is not only about those Christmases without a present . . . , those several days when she was forced to sleep on the floor in the kitchen of her own house after being beaten and spat on her face by her father. It is also not only about the day when she, looking for a new life with a man she was in love with, left everything behind just to be abandoned one day later in an unknown town, and unwittingly pregnant. Nor is it about the day when she left her two-month-old baby boy with her parents and came from Mexico to the United States with a husband, both undocumented, crossing the desert, promising to herself that she would be back no later than in six months, fifteen years having passed since. Finally, it is not only about the physical, psychological and sexual abuse she has gone through nearly every day since the beginning of her marriage.

Today, she is not telling me facts but sharing her journey. She is allowing herself to express emotions which have been repressed for such a long time. Her crying comes from the depth of her soul.

I am touched and overwhelmed. The voice of a former professor comes to my consciousness to help. She used to say that in order to effectively help our clients we had to take some distance from their emotions. I try really

[Haworth co-indexing entry note]: "Poverty, Crisis and Resilience of Spirit." Cifuentes, Mauricio. Co-published simultaneously in *Journal of Poverty* (The Haworth Press, Inc.) Vol. 8, No. 4, 2004, pp. 125-128; and: *Poverty and Inequality in the Latin American-U.S. Borderlands: Implications of U.S. Interventions* (ed: Keith M. Kilty, and Elizabeth A. Segal) The Haworth Press, Inc., 2004, pp. 125-128. Single or multiple copies of this article are available for a fee from The Haworth Document Delivery Service [1-800-HAWORTH, 9:00 a.m. - 5:00 p.m. (EST). E-mail address: docdelivery@haworthpress.com].

http://www.haworthpress.com/web/JPOV
Digital Object Identifier: 10.1300/J134v08n04_08

hard to do so though this day I just want to cry with Concepcion. Finally, the session is over.

My individual supervision session and the peer supervision group that week are the spaces to ventilate my pain, anger, and confusion. My prayers these last days comprise plenty of questions. Nevertheless, all the time a sense of hope is present as a back screen. It is the certainty that there is some meaning for the suffering, hers and mine, and for my working in that place at this point in my life.

The next week, Concepcion begins the session saying she has decided "to love myself." That day she cries and smiles at the same time. Concepcion says she knows things will be better. And I do strongly believe her.

The encounter with Concepcion reflects my experience working as a Latino social worker with a community of Mexican immigrants in Chicago. Most of these immigrants we work with at Programa C.I.E.L.O. (Heaven in Spanish)–an outreach agency of Saint Anthony Hospital which belongs to Catholic Health Partners–have been oppressed for generations, have lived in extreme poverty in their country of origin and continue being poor here, have crossed the border under extreme circumstances, are undocumented, and are considered and labeled (even by themselves) as outsiders in this country. On top of this, or perhaps as part of it, they struggle with issues coming from their individual stories, marked most of the time by the consequences of alcoholism, drug addiction, domestic violence, and sexual abuse.

At the same time, these immigrants have shown and continue to show amazing levels of endurance and resilience under the most adverse circumstances. Many, many times being with clients like Concepcion, I barely understand how they have survived, and how they are still able to smile. They have an utterly perpetual hope that almost always shows up unexpectedly. This is also seen in the case of Lucia, a woman who after trying to obtain love by having sex with several men and being considered a whore even by her family, went to therapy in the midst of a crisis. Lucia's last partner had kicked her out because his wife was coming from Mexico. In one session, while crying, Lucia smiled and said, "But I know there is someone who loves me; it does not matter what I have done and this love sustains me." I asked who that person was, expecting she would mention an aunt she had referred to as a positive, protective figure in her childhood. Instead, she said, "God."

Confronting the complex realities presented by my clients as individuals and as a community, I have gone through a profound encounter with my real self. My internal set of values and beliefs has been put under a test, and my professional ability as a social worker to offer some answers has been challenged.

At a personal level and summarizing what is almost impossible to be described, I would say that overall I have realized the divine beauty of humankind. And it provides an unreserved sense of hope–like that of my clients.

As a social worker I have confirmed and become more aware of the strong power that the environment has over human beings. I understand that there are neither simple nor single answers to the challenges presented by clients, particularly in communities like the one in which I am working. However, until now the integrative approach that we are using at C.I.E.L.O. seems to be a good way to positively respond to our clients. Julia's case exemplifies it.

It is early in the morning and my first appointment has called to cancel because of the weather. While I am preparing to catch up with some pending paper work, the secretary of C.I.E.L.O. asks me to go upstairs because there is an emergency. Julia is there crying. She is eight months pregnant, married to an alcoholic, who the night before had not come home and this morning told Julia that he had lost the money she was expecting to get to go grocery shopping, to pay rent and some other bills, and eventually to have her first appointment with an Ob/Gyn and to buy the first package of pampers for the unborn baby. Julia and her husband have another child who is almost two years old. Julia left her husband last year for three months but came back because he promised to change and because their son was missing his father. This client never went to school because her alcoholic and abusive father viewed her as just a woman and too stupid to be able to do that. She began working at the age of four to get money to provide food for herself and four younger siblings. Julia feels desperate but says she has decided to stay in the United States because here her children will have a better life than hers. And she adds, "I hope in God that I will make it."

I hear Julia and provide a holding environment for ventilation in a classic crisis intervention session. But emotional support is not enough.

We teach pre-natal classes at C.I.E.L.O. and right after our conversation, I introduce Julia to one of the educators in charge of those classes. She not only explains the curriculum and signs Julia in, but also asks for her needs and offers to get some help. Indeed, when Julia goes to her first pre-natal class the next week, she receives baby clothes, some blankets and a car seat.

Julia has no idea that she can apply for kid care being undocumented and therefore allowing her to receive medical care for free. After talking with the pre-natal educator, I introduce Julia to our kid care coordinator. The forms are filled out and some phone calls to Springfield are made trying to speed the process by taking into account that our client is almost ready to deliver her baby. Julia receives her card before the baby is born.

Julia does not know how to navigate the system and to find a good Spanish-speaking doctor. Our nurse, with whom the client talks after being with the kid care coordinator, offers Julia some options. Julia makes her decision and an appointment is set immediately. She is still seeing the same doctor.

Since Julia is the daughter and the wife of alcoholics, we offer her a referral for a group in the community that provides support to its members and every semester chooses a topic to work on. Currently it is how to survive the alcoholism in parents, spouses and other significant people.

Julia's life is still very difficult, but her sense of hope now has concrete expressions and she looks very different than the helpless woman who came to C.I.E.L.O. one day early in the morning.

While contributing to shape better lives for my clients, I am making my own life much happier. As a novice social worker looking to provide a holding environment for my mental health clients, I have found in C.I.E.L.O. a place offering a holistic response to their needs. As a result, I am also becoming a more integrated human being.

Index

Aponte, Carmen I., 59
Apoyo Familiar anti-poverty program
(Colombia), 54*n. 1*

Batista, Fulgencio, 120
Bolsa Escola scholarship program
(Brazil), 54*n. 1*
Borderlands poverty and inequality, 2-3
"borderlands" terminology, 3
See also specific country
Brazil, 2
Burwell, Rebecca, 75

Calakmul biosphere Reserve. *See*
Southern Mexico, new rural
poverty
Cash transfer programs. *See* Progresa
Program (Mexico)
Castro, Fidel, 120
CEH (Commission for Historical
Clarification, Guatemala),
15-16
Chacón, Lidia Amparo Santos, 18
Chile, 2
Church of the Word, 14, 28*n. 6*
Cifuentes, Mauricio, 125
Civil disobedience. *See* Puerto Rico,
U.S. Navy *vs.* Vieques
Columbia, 2
Commission for Historical
Clarification (CEH,
Guatemala), 15-16
Committee for the Rescue and
Development of Vieques
(CRPDV), 68
Costa Rica, 21

CRPDV (Committee for the Rescue
and Development of
Vieques), 68
Cuba
as borderland, 3
gender issues, 4
immigration issues, 3
immigration story, 119-123
independence, 61
refugees from, 5
revolution, Fidel Castro regime, 120
Roosevelt Corollary, Monroe
Doctrine, 2
trade embargo, 4,120
US intervention in, 2,4-5
See also Cuba, economic hardship
Cuba, economic hardship
dollar economy, 75,79 81-83,87,
91-92,94
embargo (U.S.), 78-79,84,120
food, 75,76,77-78,82,85-86,89,
90-91,94
gendered struggle,
76-77,80,85,89-91,94
government subsidies, 75,76,77,
89-91,91-93,94
household networks, 75,84-87
mothers, women, 75,80,89-91
multigenerational family help,
84-87,94
the Revolution, 78,94
"Special Period," 78,79,85
summary regarding, 75,94
survival strategies, 91-94
trans-continental family relations,
87-89,94
working in the street, 80-83, 94

BOOK ORDER FORM!

Order a copy of this book with this form or online at:
http://www.haworthpress.com/store/product.asp?sku=5459

Poverty and Inequality in the Latin American-U.S. Borderlands
Implications of U.S. Interventions

____ in softbound at $17.95 (ISBN: 0-7890-2752-6)
____ in hardbound at $24.95 (ISBN: 0-7890-2751-8)

COST OF BOOKS _____

POSTAGE & HANDLING _____
US: $4.00 for first book & $1.50
for each additional book
Outside US: $5.00 for first book
& $2.00 for each additional book.

SUBTOTAL _____

In Canada: add 7% GST. _____

STATE TAX _____
CA, IL, IN, MN, NJ, NY, OH & SD residents
please add appropriate local sales tax.

FINAL TOTAL _____
If paying in Canadian funds, convert
using the current exchange rate,
UNESCO coupons welcome.

❏ BILL ME LATER:
Bill-me option is good on US/Canada/
Mexico orders only; not good to jobbers,
wholesalers, or subscription agencies.

❏ Signature _____

❏ Payment Enclosed: $ _____

❏ PLEASE CHARGE TO MY CREDIT CARD:

❏ Visa ❏ MasterCard ❏ AmEx ❏ Discover
❏ Diner's Club ❏ Eurocard ❏ JCB

Account # _____

Exp Date _____

Signature _____
(Prices in US dollars and subject to change without notice.)

PLEASE PRINT ALL INFORMATION OR ATTACH YOUR BUSINESS CARD

Name	
Address	
City	State/Province	Zip/Postal Code
Country	
Tel	Fax
E-Mail	

May we use your e-mail address for confirmations and other types of information? ❏ Yes ❏ No We appreciate receiving
your e-mail address. Haworth would like to e-mail special discount offers to you, as a preferred customer.
We will never share, rent, or exchange your e-mail address. We regard such actions as an invasion of your privacy.

Order From Your **Local Bookstore** or Directly From
The Haworth Press, Inc. 10 Alice Street, Binghamton, New York 13904-1580 • USA
Call Our toll-free number (1-800-429-6784) / Outside US/Canada: (607) 722-5857
Fax: 1-800-895-0582 / Outside US/Canada: (607) 771-0012
E-mail your order to us: orders@haworthpress.com

For orders outside US and Canada, you may wish to order through your local
sales representative, distributor, or bookseller.
For information, see http://haworthpress.com/distributors

(Discounts are available for individual orders in US and Canada only, not booksellers/distributors.)

Please photocopy this form for your personal use.
www.HaworthPress.com

BOF05